The I of the Other

The I of the Other

*Mindfulness-based Diagnosis
and the Question of Sanity*

G. Kenneth Bradford, Ph.D.

Paragon House
St. Paul, Minnesota

First Edition 2013

Published in the United States by
Paragon House
1925 Oakcrest Avenue, Suite 7
St. Paul, MN 55113

www.ParagonHouse.com

Original cover photos by Galen Bradford

Library of Congress Cataloging-in-Publication Data

Bradford, G. Kenneth.
 The I of the other : mindfulness-based diagnosis and the question of sanity / by G. Kenneth Bradford, PhD. -- First edition.
     pages cm
 Includes bibliographical references.
 Summary: "A mindfulness-based approach to the knowing of Other minds revisions psychodiagnosis as a contemplative science, emphasizing the inter-subjective, contextual, and existential dimensions of experience. Attuning to the impulse to authenticity, basic sanity, and natural resilience are presented as alternative grounds upon which to base holistic psychologies and therapies"-- Provided by publisher.
 ISBN 978-1-55778-907-5 (pbk. : alk. paper) 1. Existential psychotherapy. 2. Phenomenological psychology. 3. Psychotherapist and patient. I. Title.
 RC489.E93B73 2013
 616.89'14--dc23

                              2013020511

Manufactured in the United States of America
10 9 8 7 6 5 4 3 2 1

The paper used in this publication meets the minimum requirements of American National Standard for Information Sciences—Permanence of Paper for Printed Library Materials, ANSIZ39.48-1984.

Contents

Additional Endorsements

"In this remarkable gem of a book, Kenneth Bradford draws upon and synthesizes ideas from existential phenomenology, Buddhism, and experience-near psychotherapy en route to a holistic and fully contextualized approach to psychodiagnostic and therapeutic practice. Bradford achieves no less than a definitive emancipation of psychological practice from the prevailing grip of Cartesian dualisms."

—*Robert D. Stolorow, Ph.D., author of* World, Affectivity, Trauma:
Heidegger and Post-Cartesian Psychoanalysis

"The timeliness of Ken Bradford's new book is astounding. With the arrival of the *DSM-5,* the American Psychological Association's commitment to having psychology be viewed as a science comparable to technology, engineering, and mathematics, and the echoed apocalyptic hoof beats of scientism, Bradford's book offers us multiple rays of hope in the midst of the danger of the soul becoming extinct in practices of care. Bradford challenges devoutly held presumptions of what diagnosis, assessment, empiricism, sanity, and the good life mean. His contemplative and phenomenological approach to the diagnostic process upends traditional pieces of procedural furniture so that a recovery of the being of diagnosis can occur, and do so from a multidisciplinary perspective. This book is applicable for diagnosticians, psychopathologists, and those interested in an integrated approach to psychology and spirituality from a Buddhist perspective on both a novice and expert level—a true accomplishment in writing for Bradford, which is mirrored by the content so helpful to us all. Finally, truth is spoken to power, and done so in a contemplative-phenomenological way."

—*Todd DuBose, Ph.D., Associate Professor*
The Chicago School of Professional Psychology

"Ken Bradford's recent reflections on the diagnostic moment in psychotherapy gathered in *The I of the Other* are an important anodyne to the hegemony of the psychiatric system of nosology (the *DSM*). They appear at just the right moment, when the latest iteration of *DSM* (5, 2013) is being vigorously contested by professional psychologists and the public. Bradford introduces readers to the phenomenological perspective and method of seeing through—that is, diagnosing in the original sense of the word—the meaning of existential suffering, in contrast to merely completing a checklist of behaviors and inevitably unauthenticatable reports of experience that is the method of traditional psychiatric diagnosis. If we must diagnose, the new means of going about it Bradford develops here is one that is attuned to the being-human of those who consult and sit with those of us who are psychotherapists."

—*Miles Groth, Ph.D., Professor of Psychology, Wagner College, New York and an existential analyst in private practice in New York City*

"Bradford describes a holistic, experiential approach to diagnosis and treatment with a clarity and rigor that I find rare in the literature. Crisply written and eminently readable, this book is intellectually stimulating and thought-provoking, and a skillfully worked clinical vignette gives it great hands-on appeal as well. Those familiar with incorporating mindfulness practice in their work will find in Bradford's approach a way to take it deeper, from a mere technique to a container and soul of the work itself.

Bradford presents a view of sanity not defined by culturally shaped traits or qualities or any content whatsoever but by openness and connectedness within the self as well as toward the world and other people. Such a view avoids reductionism into neurophysiological or social constructs and is uniquely relevant and responsive to the challenges of our times."

—*Kaisa Puhakka, Ph.D.*
Professor of Psychology, California Institute of Integral Studies
Former Editor of The Journal of Transpersonal Psychology

Preface and Acknowledgments

This book emerged out of a graduate course on psychological assessment and diagnosis I have taught over a period of almost twenty years. Recognizing at the outset that the *Diagnostic and Statistical Manual of Mental Disorders* (*DSM*) is ill-designed to inform and guide experientially-rigorous psychotherapy practices, this course presented an alternative phenomenological-contemplative approach to diagnosis that is more in sync with the humanistic-transpersonal-somatically-keyed therapy practices taught in the Graduate School of Holistic Studies at John F. Kennedy University. At its beginnings, the course exclusively applied the phenomenological research method to clinical assessment. As far as I know, this was a first attempt to apply the phenomenological methodology to clinical psychodiagnosis.

It was my good fortune to have had Amedeo Giorgi direct my doctoral dissertation research (Bradford, 1989), in which I learned how the rigor of the phenomenological method met and exceeded that of the scientific method for the purpose of understanding human subjectivity as a phenomenon of subjectivity. Inspired to share this knowledge, I originally limited the course to the method of descriptive phenomenology. Over time, my therapeutic orientation leaned increasingly in a contemplative direction. Reflecting this shift, the course morphed from "A Phenomenological Approach" to "A Mindfulness-Based Approach," situating phenomenological knowing within the broader field of contemplative science. As *mindfulness-based*, the approach orients psychological knowing both to the increasingly prominent vocabulary of *mindfulness* in the field as well as marking the slippage of the formal phenomenological research methodology into the decidedly less formal, "on the fly" kind of empathically-keyed, inter-subjective inquiry that is more true to actual therapeutic exchanges. This slippage of the research protocol into the spontaneity of therapeutic conversation allows for an enhanced ability to linger in as-yet-undefined felt dimensions of attunement so vital to depth psychotherapy.

This evolution accompanied my increasing discomfort over the years with the audacity, if not arrogance, involved in presuming anyone can accurately know the mind of an Other. It is difficult enough to understand the complexity of one's own mind! I have lived enough life and practiced enough therapy to have succumbed both to the hubris that thinks on the one hand, I (genius that I am) can know more about you than you do yourself, and, the self-doubt that thinks on the other hand, I (idiot that I am) can know nothing about you that you don't already know yourself. Recognizing the pitfalls of each extreme, I have come to realize that the most powerful knowledge of an Other is less *what* I think I know about a person than *how* I hold those thoughts. The important point is less the knowledge I think I have or lack about someone than how I reflect that knowing and not-knowing. That is, to what extent is my knowledge of another person a projection of my own prejudices and to what extent is it an accurate perception of the Other? *How* I hold another person in my thoughts and feelings influences what I *make of* that person, which always includes both the knowledge I have as well as that which I lack.

However, in the urgency to make sense of someone and their situation—so to feel more oriented ourselves as psychologists, we tend to ignore what we lack and the fact that the sense we do make will always be incomplete. The all-too-human tendency is to cling to something, either to the surety of what we know or to the vertigo of our unknowing, while ignoring all else. In *making something of* someone, "sizing them up," we shatter the Otherness of their I by constructing an image of our own and nominating that image as their I in place of their Otherness. Instead of allowing *ourselves* to be shaken or even shattered (following Emmanual Levinas) in risking a genuine encounter with another person, we both absent ourselves and ignore the mysterious elusiveness of our partner in the exchange. This absence and that ignorance invariably results in a diminished awareness and lack of humility, courage, and compassion, thus obscuring both the other person and the fullness of our own experience in being with him or her.

A more vital, thorough, and nuanced approach to the knowing of Other minds inheres in *the capacity to be present to and with the uncanny otherness of the Other* without reducing them to the familiar categories of our own apperception. Identifying this approach as "mindfulness-based" reflects the fact that this is more a meditative practice than a conceptually-based assessment. Contemplative science is less concerned about arriving at an objective conclusion than in maintaining fidelity to what is still always emerging in the inter-subjective field of the unfolding present moment.

This book would not exist were it not for Ray Greenleaf, former Chair of the Holistic Counseling Psychology program at John F. Kennedy University, who encouraged me to teach mindfulness meditation as a foundational practice for psychological assessment. More crucially, were it not for my students, too numerous to name, who enthusiastically embraced the practices of mindful inquiry and engaged in spirited discussions critiquing the *DSM*, I surely would not have felt it important to write more responsibly about these topics. One requirement of the course is to adopt a daily practice of mindfulness meditation and to personally examine its effects. It is worthy of note that a disproportionately high number of students went on to tell me, sometimes years after graduation, that this assignment of personal meditation, which I commend as a form of daily "psychic hygiene" analogous to "dental hygiene," was one of, if not *the,* most important thing they gained from their graduate education. They felt this was important not only for honing their perceptive diagnostic faculties, but also for deepening their own self-understanding and self-acceptance.

My sincere gratitude goes to John Prendergast, Kaisa Puhakka, and Art Giacalone for their valuable feedback and encouragement in the preparation of the journal articles upon which this book is based. Although I have edited and added to all the articles in the preparation of this book, Chapters One and Two originally appeared in the *Journal of Humanistic Psychology* (2010, *50*(3), 335-350); Chapter Three was published in the *Journal of Transpersonal Psychology* (2009, 1*41*(2), 121-138); Chapter Four also appeared in the *Journal of Transpersonal Psychology* (2012, 44(2), 224-239); and Chapter Five was first published in *Voices: The art and science of psychotherapy* (2002, 38(4), 52-58). My thanks to the publishers of these journals for granting permission to include that material in this book.

Introduction

In the study of ideas it is necessary to remember that insistence on hardheaded clarity issues from sentimental feeling, as it were a mist, cloaking the perplexities of fact. Our reasonings grasp at straws for premises and float on gossamers for deductions.

—Alfred North Whitehead

Psychological theories, diagnostic schemas, and therapeutic practices emerge from a knowledge of mind and assumptions regarding human nature which are often tacit and taken for granted, remaining unexamined. For instance, the theory of mind of contemporary Psychology is based on the materialistic principles of empirical science. According to its Cartesian foundations, scientific empiricism defines mind, or "I" (*res cogitans*), as something separate and distinct from the Otherness of both the body and the world (*res extensa*). The mind, or subjective knower (*cogito*), can neither, according to Descartes, know itself or itself be known. The most that can be said, as Descartes famously declared is, *cogito, ergo sum*, "I think, therefore I am." Human *being* is thus reduced to a thinker which recedes into an invisible interiority from which it peers out to survey an exterior object world (*res extensa*). The world in this sense includes all manner of physical, social, and even mental objects.

The scientific revolution replaced the caprice of personal opinion and the dogmatic religious assertions of the Christian Middle Ages with the measurable objectivity of material truths. Within this empiricist worldview, that which can be discerned as true is only that which can be objectively measured, which is always some *thing* or *matter*, separate and distinct from the observing mind. The perceptive human subject is thus irrevocably divided from the objects of the world. This results in the thought and practices of conventional Psychology being formed and informed according to a fundamental subject-object split.

As the ostensible subject matter of psychology, *mind* is conceived to be both disembodied and decontextualized. Any empirical scientific knowledge of the mind must be arrived at from outside the knowing mind itself. This necessarily results in a psychology that objectifies subjective experience, transforming mind and mental events into materialistic entities. This conception of the detached mind inevitably confuses and misguides those forms of psychological practice which value holistic approaches to the understanding of human nature and the treatment of mental suffering. The differences between a psychology based on the model of a detached mind versus holistic approaches emphasizing a contextualized and embodied mind are nowhere more definitive than in the diagnosis of psychopathology. How mental suffering is diagnosed determines how that *pathos* is understood and what kinds of treatment methods are deemed appropriate to treat it.

It is worthwhile to examine the basic assumptions of Psychology so to better evaluate the appropriateness of those suppositions for the practical diagnostic and therapeutic tasks at hand. This means, after clearly recognizing the dualistic presumptions of scientific empiricism, we must distinguish these from other, less dualistic or non-dualistic assumptions upon which to ground a psychology more appropriate to the exquisitely subjective nature of human being in the world.

To proceed, we will primarily draw upon the orientations of Existential-Phenomenology, Buddhist thought and practice, and experience-near psychotherapy. These disciplines are akin insofar as they each advocate *holistic*— in the sense of contextualized, embodied, and relational— approaches to psychological knowledge. Each of these orientations challenge the dominance of Cartesian empiricism and its privileging of objectivity, which, by ignoring the nature of subjectivity itself, can lead to subtle and not-so-subtle forms of self-other estrangement and dehumanization. In addition to protesting the experience-distant, objectifying tendencies of empiricism and its diagnostic prejudices, it is incumbent upon alternative psychologies to clarify why it is preferable to proceed in an experience-near, holistic direction. Since any psychotherapeutic engagement begins with getting to know the mind, or psychic disposition, of another person, it is appropriate that a holistic revisioning of psychology begin by rethinking the foundational knowing we refer to as clinical diagnosis.

Empirical Science and the *DSM*

We ought not forget that the field of Psychology is in its infancy, and its current empiricist framing of psychopathology is no more solid than sand at the ocean's edge. While we like to think that the findings of conventional Science form the pinnacle of empirical knowledge, including psychological truths, on what basis can this hegemony be claimed? There is a vibrant tradition in the West, from Wilhelm Dilthey and William James to Existential philosophers, cultural anthropologists, and social, humanistic, and transpersonal psychologists that has vigorously challenged the appropriateness of applying the Scientific Method to the *human* sciences, judging it to be inadequate for understanding the complexities and subtleties of human experience. (See Boss, 1983; Ferrer, 2002; Gadamer, 1982/1960; Giorgi, 1970; Husserl, 1970/1954; James, 1922/1912; Merleau-Ponty 1963/1942; Szasz, 1974; and Van den Berg, 1972, but to name a few.) This broad contra-tradition advocates methods of study that are more able to accord to our uniquely subjective and inter-subjective nature. As the Buddhist scholar, Andrew Olendzki (2012) succinctly puts it,

We can study the structure and function of the brain's neurons, transmitters, and other components, and we can study behavior. But the subjective phenomenology of human experience seems fundamentally inaccessible to existing methods of objective inquiry. There is no instrument that can measure what it feels like to have an experience; there is no data set that can adequately record the nuances of a felt sensation; there is no theorem that can encompass the many idiosyncrasies of a unique human being. It may be that no third-person explanation can ever address the phenomenon of selfhood, insofar as it will always be imbedded in a first-person perspective. (p.82)

Beyond the modern Western tradition in which Psychology has existed as a discrete discipline for less than two centuries, traditions of depth psychology in the East, such as Vedanta, Buddhism, and Taoism, have been developed, applied, and tested over millennia. The knowledge of these more mature sciences of mind, especially in regard to mental *health* and the evolutionary potentialities of human being, dwarf that of Western Psychology.

Contrary to the objectivizing catechism of the scientific method, Eastern psychological sciences conceive of mind as a subject matter best accessed through subjectively-attuned meditative approaches. These approaches utilize experiential methods of exploration and verifiability that endeavor to understand particular subjective *states* of mind (whether expansive or contracted), as well as the *nature* of mind states and subjectivity itself. More fundamental than any nosology of mental states or psychology of developmental stages, is the ontology (nature) of mental states and stages. Psychology might begin, and I would say, is ethically bound to begin, by considering what it is that constitutes the basic, essential subject matter of psychology. The ontological question asks, What is *it* that suffers, exalts, and otherwise experiences the various and particular mental and emotional states that arise, persist, and pass away?

Regarding this question, the field of Psychology is strangely mute. Not having a clear understanding of the actual nature of its subject matter, which for Psychology should include a comprehension of the nature of sanity, we are left, at best, with notions of sanity-insanity which are limited to specific cultural contexts. As Michel Foucault points out, this strictly relative knowledge reveals more about the constructs of the particular social context in which madness (and sanity) is understood than it does about the psychological nature of madness (or sanity) per se.

A Brief History of Madness

In considering European history, Foucault (1965) found conceptions of madness to have varied widely over the last several centuries. In the Middle Ages, madness was often considered to be a form of demonic possession, supposedly caused by the temptation to indulge in sins that might send the sinner into an everlasting damnation. In the late Middle Ages, madness seems to have morphed from strictly being a manifestation of vague moral laxity into a kind of awe-full folly, transporting the "fool" beyond the apparent world into a mysterious otherworldliness in which he appeared to *lose* his mind.

During the 15th and 16th Centuries, European cities and towns had an uneasy relationship to madness in which they would cast out the madmen and women in their midst, exiling them on the notorious "ships of fools." These ships would carry their mad cargo along the rivers and canals of Europe, sometimes randomly dropping the "fools" off in distant towns. The ships would also disembark passengers at Christian pilgrimage sites or monasteries, which would find a place for madwomen and men within the spiritual life of those communities. During this pre-scientific period, which was attuned both toward the visible, sensory world as well as toward the invisibilities of the extrasensory, spiritual world, madness was seen as a mystery among mysteries and often respected as such. Even though local communities banished fools from their townships, madness was understood as a spiritual—rather than psychological—manifestation, a "being touched." During this era, it was not necessarily clear whether a person so touched was a good thing: the madness being perhaps a divine affliction from God, or a bad thing such as a demonic possession. Especially for the devout layperson or spiritual pilgrim, madness could evoke a sense of awe, and in keeping with the practice of Christian charity (*caritas*), was likely to inspire spiritual seekers to relate to a mad person with a measure of forbearance, if not kindness.

Concurrently in the medieval world, and more stridently into the 17th Century, there emerged "lunatic asylums," such as Bedlam, in which the insane were incarcerated. The purpose of these "madhouses" was confinement and restraint. Contrary to the earlier response of deporting the insane: sending them away somewhere over the rainbow, or at least over the horizon, there developed the response of locking them up. While the mad may have lost their minds, the culture was increasingly not at a loss as to how to respond to such lostness. In contrast to spiritual awe in the face of madness, this increasingly secular attitude was more focused on suppression and containment.

With the rise of hospitals and related detention centers throughout the 17th and 18th Centuries, mad persons came to be lumped together with criminals, vagrants, and the disenfranchised, all of whom shared the common fault of being poor. During this period, idleness was considered the mother of all evils. Those without work were obviously not observing the Protestant work ethic and those who were found begging or indolent on the street were indiscriminately imprisoned together during the rise of the industrial era. Madness was seen as a variant of a particular and unfortunately widespread double laxity: a lack of industriousness as well as a flaunting display of *unreason.* This period of the Age of Reason, in which rationality assumes a prime value, finds displays of unreason to be immoral, a display of a kind of sub-humanity, or animality. Rather than being seen as a sickness to which some medicine might be applied, insanity was seen to be a moral failing requiring correction through discipline, punishment, and even brutality, such as lashings and other physical degradations. As a form of bestiality, madness was seen as having a wild, untamed vitality, displaying a bold and threatening freedom expressing an excess of passion. Even today, this equivalence of madness and passion endures, as we readily speak of being "mad" when we find ourselves angry. We speak of the emotion itself as crazy rather than our fixation on it, our compulsion to it, or our (perhaps unskillful) expression of it.

Into the Victorian era of the 19th Century, the suppression of emotionality was especially concentrated in women, who were (and are?) widely conceived to be the more sensitive, more emotional sex. Conceived as a weakness, or even a kind of deformity, emotional sensitivity led women in particular to be considered more prone to manifestations of unreason. Of course, men likewise suffered from the mandate of emotional suppression, including of their vulnerability and felt needs for giving and receiving expressions of tenderness. But while men had ready access to alcohol abuse and sexual debauchery to blunt the suffering of their emotional sensitivity, women at large did not have such access.

The case of hysteria is particularly informative, pointing as it does to a malady of the uterus. Considered earlier to be an insanity caused by uterine bad spirits coursing through the nerves, it began to be construed as a "pathology of imagination" revealing that some women tended toward oversensitivity in having both too much feeling and too much imagination.

Hysteria increasingly was conceived to be an irritability of the physiological nervous system, along with mania and melancholia. The conception of madness as a specifically neurological illness rose to prominence, and medical treatments developed. Seen as diseases of the nerves, treatments for insanity often involved various soothing treatments to calm nervous irritabilities, so to mollify emotional upwellings and the body's mute expressions of nervous distress, which included the various paralyses common to conversion hysterias of the time.

It is only toward the end of the 19th Century, with the rise of psychiatry, that madness was conceived as a specifically mental kind of illness. Freud, first educated as a neurologist and then transforming into the first psychoanalyst, marks this transition. Adhering to the empiricist worldview, the medical approach to "nervous disease" conceived it either as a neuro-physiological problem or as a specifically psychological malady. In either case, it is seen as an objectively existing manifestation (*res extensa*).

Continuing on this basis, during the 20th Century, an era of unbridled techno-mechanization, the conception of mental *illness* morphed into that of mental *disorder*. Even though mental disorders continue to be construed as disattached medical illnesses, the notion of "disorder" amplifies the sense of the individual faultiness of an isolated mind as well as the implicit assumption that there must be a sane, but unspecified, "order" to psychological life that has gone astray. These morphing construals of madness, including the interminable revisions of the American Psychiatric Association's *Diagnostic and Statistical Manual of Mental Disorders (DSM)*, reveal the context-bound relativity of diagnostic formulae. In spite of this strictly relative understanding, contemporary psychodiagnoses (and the treatments it empowers) presume to have a dependable scientific *validity* and *reliability* that is not relative to shifting cultural winds.

There is a fundamental problem—scientific, medical, and existential—when a social construction of mental dysfunction, such as the *DSM*, is presumed to have authority and validity beyond its social context. Yet, this is exactly the claim that the *DSM*, which presents itself as a valid instrument of objective truth generalizable to anyone at anytime, has the audacity to make.

This is the problem of *projection*, when we see the Other, something or someone, without recognizing that what or who we see is distorted by our own imaginative construction of them. Projection is the common error of de-contextualizing our knowledge of the world, seeing the Other as an extension of our own prejudices. This error is so common because we lose touch with the nature of our mind which has the capacity to either project or not project its constructs onto others and Otherness. Being out of touch with mind's imaginative nature, we become captivated by the mind's projections without recognizing 1) that this is happening and 2) that we are the one doing it. Thus we imagine we see the world, including other people and our own self-image, as objectively existing, separated from our envisioning of it/them. The worldview of empirical science reifies and exalts this phenomenon of dualistic vision by taking the observer (*res cogitans*) out of the field of observation.

Variations of how madness is understood over time and in different places reveal something about the plasticity of the human mind's ability to make sense (and nonsense) within a variety of contexts. However, merely noting these variations reveals nothing about the nature of the mind's plasticity itself.

It must be conceded that Psychology does not (yet) have an agreed-upon understanding of the basic nature of its own, inherently malleable, subject matter. Lacking this fundamental knowledge, how valid can its presumably objective diagnoses possibly be? To presume that a construal of mental disorders, as codified in the *DSM* for instance, is true in any kind of fundamental way, particularly as a form of subjectively-rigorous knowledge, is mere superstition. Given its widespread acceptance and inordinate power both in the fields of Psychology and in the culture at large, it is important to expose the fundamental fallacies of the *DSM*, which forms the focus of Chapter One. Chapter Two proceeds to sketch several general criteria for grounding and guiding holistic and contemplative scientific approaches to psychodiagnosis.

Mindfulness-Based: Toward a Contemplative Science

Inquiring into the nature of mind states invites a reversal of Descartes' conclusion, "I think, therefore I am" into, "I am, therefore I think." Especially in the knowing of other minds, recognizing the merit of this reversal immediately shifts the power dynamic between doctor and patient. Allowing that clinical theories and diagnostic constructs are not absolute, but relative to particular circumstances, stimulates a respect both for what one does not know as well as for the Otherness of the other person. At the very least, this respect engenders an attitude of humility and may well elicit a relational hospitality on the part of the therapist.

In order to adequately inquire into the nature of the mind it is imperative to begin in a way that recognizes the necessity of according to that nature. Ontological accordance requires accessing the capability for *being-present* to self and other. *Mindfulness* is simply the capacity for being attentive, such that it is possible to be more fully present in the here and now. Only in being undistractedly attentive is it possible to pause long enough to disentangle unconscious projections from inter-subjective perceptions.

I have found it advantageous to intertwine the contemplative approaches of Buddhism and Phenomenology so to form a conducive starting point for accessing and deploying mindful attunement. Buddhism has evolved both meditative methods and conceptual understandings of the nature of mind and mental states which are second to none. Phenomenology is among the most rigorous of Western approaches offering a experience-near method of subjective and inter-subjective inquiry. Based on the assumption that the mind is a *phenomenon* to explore rather than an object to identify, phenomenology offers an able method through which to attune to complexities and subtleties of subjective experience. Additionally, phenomenological thought has sophisticated understandings of mind and holistic views of being in the world which can be taken as felicitous points of departure to guide inquiry into existential awareness. In both traditions, the primary method of cognizance is meditative and subjectively-keyed rather than conceptually mediated and object-bound.

As a phenomenologically-inspired practice, psychoanalysis has convincingly shown that conceptual thought is insufficient for coming to a nuanced understanding of mind. Conceptuality discriminates, focusing on one thing at a time, marking differences and making separations, elaborating a rationally-bound vision of thises versus thats. However, the conscious motivation for making a distinction and then choosing to focus on a particular *this* is often co-determined by an unconscious motivation of *not* wanting to focus on a troubling *that*. Psychoanalysis well-understands that conscious rationality is not wholly rational at all, but is co-directed by non-rational, emotionally-influenced strands of intentionality. In order to account for the emotional and not-fully-conscious dimensionality of mind, it is necessary to gain access to mind's non-rationality. Various methods of depth psychotherapy, including evenly-suspended attention, free association, active imagination, felt sensing, empathic attunement, and mindfulness, each aim to facilitate access to the wholeness of the mind in both its conceptual and non-conceptual dimensions.

For ease of discussion, I am using "mindfulness," "meditative," "contemplative," and "non-conceptual awareness" as interchangeable synonyms referring to experience-near inquiry. Used in an admittedly broad-brush manner, these terms all refer to an approach that seeks to access mind *from the inside*, subjectively and inter-subjectively, rather than observing it in empiricist fashion from the outside. Chapter Three re-visions diagnosis as a phenomenological practice grounded in meditative awareness.

The prime directive of contemplative science is to understand the mind of an Other, or oneself, as it reveals itself on its own terms and in its own time, rather than by forcing the Other, or oneself, to conform to a preconceived theory and pre-constructed categories. Contemplative inquiry appropriate to holistic approaches presents a challenge to the diagnostician and psychotherapist beyond that of simply learning another theoretical reference system. Even though the capacity for mindful attention, "listening with the third ear," is arguably the most essential skill for the practice of any depth psychology, it is strangely under-taught in much of the field, including post-doctoral training institutes. While the learning of conceptual reference systems is not so difficult, loosening the grip with which we cling to reference systems challenges us on an emotional level to bear the openness and vulnerability of non-conceptual presence, which is rather more difficult.

The practice of mindfulness is a skill that, once learned and consistently practiced, tends to mature over time, granting the practitioner greater access to the subtleties and complexities of subjective/intersubjective experience that often remain invisible to discursive thinking. It is the aim of this book to aid and abet the initiative of folding contemplative awareness more surely into the diagnostic practices of psychology.

The Nature of Sanity

On the basis of mindful awareness, Chapter Four differentiates between relative sanity, recognized as a social construction (Berger & Luckmann, 1967) conditioned by the cultural context which construes it, and *unconditioned sanity*, which is the foundational capacity for the construction, deconstruction, and reconstruction of social constructs. While the social construction of psychological attitudes is important to recognize, it reveals nothing about the unconstructed nature of cognizance itself which allows for mental and social constructions. In seeking to comprehend the essential subject matter of Psychology: *psyche,* or *psychic,* the notion that there could be such a thing as an essential human nature, or basic sanity, is certainly controversial. In the post-modern way of thinking, in which all knowledge, being constructed, is strictly relative to its context, the possibility of *essential sanity, which is an unconstructed, trans-contextual, primordial intelligence,* may be seen to be idealistic, improbable, or a naive regression to religious metaphysics.

To this worthy objection, I would say it is first of all necessary to observe the difference between conceptually constructed (ontic) forms of knowledge and the ontological capacity for knowing. In regard to determinations of sanity/insanity, Chapters 3-5 consider how identifying with transient *states of mind* lead one to get caught up in emotional states and mental formulations, perhaps to the point of getting lost in them, thus losing (touch with) one's mind (itself). Identifying with the mind's productions and fixating on mental-emotional constructs takes one away from the inherently intelligent and naturally resilient nature of mind. In contrast to the lostness of relative sanity and insanity, in which one is entranced by the mind's projections, including if those projections are shared and validated in a consensual reality, is the usually unrecognized resilience of basic sanity.

Drawing primarily upon Buddhist knowledge, Chapters Four and Five endeavor to upgrade Psychology's impoverished understanding of the nature of mind in pointing to the intrinsic healthiness of unconditional awareness. The calm wakefulness of unconstructed and unconstructing presence is a bearing that is attuned to the inherent openness of its own nature and thus to the unconfined, unfixated, and non-conceptual cognizance which arises effortlessly therein. This *natural resilience* is the topic of the final chapter, and will be discussed as the optimal groundless ground upon which to base authentically robust, subjectively nuanced, and inter-relationally situated psychodiagnostic and therapeutic practices.

CHAPTER ONE

Fundamental Flaws of the DSM

*It is not the victory of science that distinguishes our nineteenth century, but the victory of the **scientific method** over science.*

—Friedrich Nietzsche

The method of science is nothing but the securing of the calculability of nature.

—Martin Heidegger

Psychological diagnosis informed by the *Diagnostic and Statistical Manual of Mental Disorders* (*DSM*) presumes to make valid and reliable knowledge claims regarding the pathological nature of other minds. As a matter of pragmatics, psychological professionals exercise this bold knowledge and deploy its formidable power on a daily basis. The culture at large relies on this privileged knowledge to distinguish between abnormal mental diseases and normal states of mind. As we know, the impact of a clinical diagnosis can be far-reaching, not only in terms of dictating medical treatment, but also in terms of shaping a person's psychological identity, both in their own eyes and in the eyes of others. So it is important to consider: How accurate is the *DSM* in making diagnoses?

In addition, experiential therapies, transpersonal psychologies, and spiritual disciplines go beyond merely distinguishing between normal and abnormal mental states by discerning subtle, complex, and exceptional states of mind that are neither conventionally "normal" nor categorically "pathological." Whether making a rough distinction between normal and abnormal or making a more nuanced assessment of the subtleties and complexities of an experiential process, it is incumbent upon therapists and spiritual guides to consider how truly and thoroughly it is possible to know the mind of an Other.

In general, psychiatric diagnosis has been problematic for humanistic and transpersonally-oriented psychologies and experientially-keyed psychotherapies for quite sometime. Not only have American founders of Humanistic and Transpersonal Psychology, such as, Maslow (1971), Rogers (1961), and Bugental (1965), stridently opposed pathologizing diagnosis, the anti-psychiatry movement has been outspoken about the "vocabulary of denigration" (Quoted in Laing, 1960, p.27) inherent in pathology-keyed diagnostic discourse. European philosophers and psychologists have likewise criticized objectivizing and dehumanizing psychodiagnosis, and still more importantly have challenged the empirical science paradigm upon which this discourse is based (For instance, Binswanger, 1963; Boss, 1983; Husserl, 1970/1954; Laing, 1960 & 1969; and Merleau-Ponty, 1963/1942.).

As early as 1894, Dilthey pointed out that the empirical scientific method that studies the physical world by dissecting an object into its constituent elements is inappropriate for the study of human subjectivity. As Van den Berg (1972) reports, "In [Dilthey's] opinion, the essential characteristic of the psychic aspect of human life is that it is a *totality* not a collection of elements" (p.126, my emphasis). He goes on to declare, "The aim of psychology is the rendering of a totality….[it] is to observe, to comprehend, then to render explicit…what was at first seen vaguely in the first comprehension" (p.127). The way to understand the *whole person* is to encounter that person as they reveal themselves rather than construing the person according to one's own preconceived categories. Dilthey recognized knowledge that most accurately reveals a whole person proceeds as a *process* of explicating what is at first only seen vaguely. This holistic, process-based orientation has been generally understood as a phenomenological, or *experiential,* approach, which was first applied to psychology as early as 1913 by Karl Jaspers (p.128). In America, William James first published *Essays in Radical Empiricism* in 1912, in which he advocated for an experience-near *radical* empiricism that is "unlike so much of the *halfway empiricism* that is current under the name of positivism" (p.vii, my emphasis). Since that time, there have been continuing efforts to reconceive psychology as a *human science* utilizing qualitative and holistic approaches sensitive to the complexities of subjective experiencing. (See Boss, 1982/1963; Ferrer, 2002; Giorgi, 1970; May, Angel & Ellenberger, 1958; Schneider, Bugental & Pierson, 2001; and Valle & Halling, 1989; but to name a few.) Even though these efforts to revision psychology as a *subjective* science, based on vastly different grounds from the "halfway empirical," *objective* sciences, have to some extent been heeded in Europe, they have not prevailed in the United States. In the U.S., the enduring power of the empirical science establishment and the diagnostic authority of its handmaiden, the *DSM*, remains king.

Generally, the various inspired efforts critiquing the *DSM* do so from outside empirical science proper. There is nothing wrong with this, especially since the most interesting part of human science critiques are often the novel alternatives they offer, be they humanistic, transpersonal, existential, systemic, feminist, or integral. However, the "outsider position" of these critiques makes it easier for those who believe that the principles and methods of empiricism are the only legitimate science, to dismiss alternative critiques as "unscientific." Thus, in the evolution of the *DSM*, alternative visions are largely disregarded as the medical diagnostic machine grinds on as a strictly empiricist instrument of classification. This leaves the growing constituency of experience-near therapeutic approaches—everything from psychoanalysis to somatic psychologies—without a clear, rigorous, and generally accepted diagnostic approach able to account for the subjective complexities of human experience. Therefore, many such therapists, in spite of serious reservations, fall back on the *DSM* as the *lingua franca* of the field. In order to substantially shift this order of things, it is necessary to expose the flaws in the *DSM* as it currently exists, both from the outside and from inside its empiricist paradigm and to conceive of viable human science alternatives.

Empirical Scientific Flaws of the DSM

The DSM is fundamentally flawed in two essential ways. As an instrument of empirical science, its facts—pathological categories—can be considered true only if they are found to be both **valid** and **reliable**. In terms of psychodiagnosis, the test of validity is a measure of whether a particular diagnosis actually exists as it is posited. The test of reliability determines whether a validly established diagnosis can be consistently recognized as the thing it is. For example, a diagnosis of depression is valid if it accurately distinguishes the abnormal disorder, "depression," be it Major Depression, Dysthymia, or another Mood Disorder, from each other as well as from normal moody states, such as sadness, mopiness, moroseness, or grief. The diagnosis is reliable if a particular depression is consistently recognized as such by various observers. On both of these crucial empirical standards the *DSM* fails, either wholly or in part. Regarding reliability, epidemiological research conducted in the 1960s and 70s showed that the diagnoses of major illnesses were unreliable over both time and across cultures (Goldstein & Goldstein, 1978, p.138-186). One study comparing psychiatric hospital admissions in New York and London in 1963 found that 77% of all New York admissions were diagnosed as having schizophrenia, whereas only 35% were so diagnosed in London that year. In addition, less than 7% of New Yorkers were diagnosed with manic-depressive disorders, while 32% of the Londoners garnered this diagnosis. This data indicates, quite darkly, an epidemic of schizophrenia in New York, but rather brightly, only scant manic-depression (Chart 1).

Chart 1: Original diagnoses of 200 hospital admissions by psychiatrists (excluding alcohol and drug admissions).

	New York	London	Ratio London:New York
Schizophrenia	76.6%	35.3%	0.46
Manic-Depressive Disorders	6.5%	32.3%	5.0
Other diagnoses	16.9%	32.4%	

However, when the psychiatric charts of these hospital admissions were re-evaluated by a conjoint team of British and American research psychiatrists, the New York diagnoses were found to be grossly mistaken. Upon re-evaluation, the rate for schizophrenia decreased from 77% to (a more British-like) 39%, while the manic-depressive diagnosis dramatically increased from 7% to 35% (close to the British rate). When the conjoint team re-evaluated the London admissions, the British diagnoses did not significantly change (Chart 2).

Chart 2: Rediagnoses of the same patients following a specification of the diagnostic criteria.

	New York	London	Ratio London:New York
Schizophrenia	39.4%	37.0%	0.94
Manic-Depressive Disorders	34.5%	30.9%	0.90
Other diagnoses	26.1%	32.1%	

This study revealed that American psychiatrists (in the post-WWII era) did not see depression when it sat in front of them, just as they did see psychosis where there was none. Based on this cross-cultural comparison, the schizophrenic epidemic in the United States at the time apparently was only happening in the minds of the diagnosticians.

Other studies investigated the reliability of diagnoses

made solely in the United States over time. One such study (Goldstein & Goldstein, 1978, p.149-151) compared original hospital diagnoses made in the 1930s to those made in the 1950s. This study found that only 28% of hospital admissions were diagnosed as schizophrenia in the 1930s, while a full 77% admissions (again) were found to have schizophrenia in the decade immediately following the second world war. As part of this study, the admission charts from both decades were rediagnosed in 1973, and from that vantage point, *both* were found to be in error! The 1973 rediagnoses found 42% of the 1930s hospital admissions to have schizophrenia, up from the original 28%, while 47% of the 1947-56 admissions were rediagnosed as schizophrenic, down from the whopping 77% (Chart 3).

Chart 3: Number of Schizophrenia cases out of 64.

	Original hospital diagnosis	Rediagnosis made in 1973
1932-41 decade	18 (28%)	27 (42%)
1947-56 decade	49 (77%)	30 (47%)

Both of these studies found psychiatric diagnoses to be notoriously unreliable. In addition, the discrepancies this research uncovered raise many still unanswered questions, including: Why might depression-era psychiatry see widespread manic-depression but hardly any schizophrenia, while the post-war era of exuberant optimism and rampant materialism saw hardly anyone depressed, but did see in its troubled citizenry an epidemic of schizophrenia?

Motivated largely by these kinds of revelations, psychiatry attempted to improve the reliability of its diagnoses by completely revising the *DSM*, resulting in the 1980 publication of the *DSM-III*. Stripping the *DSM-II* of virtually all personality theory, most notably that of psychoanalysis, including the longstanding distinction between the neuroses and the psychoses, the *DSM-III* employed strict symptom-focused diagnostic criteria. One particularly striking change was the complete disappearance of "neuroses" from the *DSM-III*. This raises the question, where did the neuroses go? Certainly they had not all been cured. Or had they? Did they ever really exist in the first place, say in the way that a hematoma or tumor exists? Or, was neurosis, either deliberately or inadvertently, being suppressed by the psychiatric establishment? Of these questions, the most compelling one to my way of thinking is that which questions the very existence of presumed psychodiagnostic categories, such as "neurosis" or "depression."

As based in the medical model, it is presumed that mental illness exists in a similar way as does physical illness. But, is it true that psychological disease, including neuroses, exist in the same way as do their physiological disease counterparts? Keep in mind that the medical model is an artifact of empirical science and construes its knowledge by dissecting a whole into its component parts. For instance, recall that physical medicine is above all based on the corpse. It is by dissecting a corpse, and gaining an understanding of the separate functions of organs and the different anatomical parts of the body that physical medicine proceeds. This is true in both medical training and medical research. Since psychological illness is likewise construed according to this empiricist vision, mental functioning is presumed to exist in the same way. But while it is possible to dissect a corpse and see the tumor or hematoma inside of it, where in the corpse is the depression, anxiety, or narcissistic personality disorder to be found? Of course, physiological psychology responds to this question by reporting as "evidence" such "hard facts" as MRI scans of the brains of chronic schizophrenics, which show their brains to be abnormally misshapen: shrunken and darkened in certain areas. But is this the "schizophrenia" illness itself? Or, is a damaged brain a *consequence* of the schizophrenia, like atrophied leg muscles are a consequence of a paraplegic spinal injury?

Obviously, physiological phenomena, which are often observable in and as parts of a physical body, are of a different order than psychological experience, which belong to, and affect, the whole of a human mind (-body). This crucial difference has been consistently ignored by empirical scientific psychology, and apparently the fundamental question concerning the *actual nature of psychological phenomena* has never seriously been considered in the development of the *DSM*. Since Psychology has not taken the time to understand the nature of its subject matter: psychological experience, misunderstandings have continued to flourish. For instance, while "neuroses" suddenly disappeared from diagnostic formulae in the *DSM-III*, in their place mental "disorders" suddenly appeared. But where did *they* come from? And, what does "disorder" actually mean anyway? Obviously, it presumes an "orderliness" to mental life that can go awry. But what exactly is baseline mental orderliness? And who is it that determines this? Since no cogent explanations are given, either of mental "order" or "disorder," how can anyone assume that "disorders"—as a fundamental explanatory framework—are any more credible than "neuroses" for accurately portraying psychological states?

Even though the new language and symptom-only focus of the *DSM-III* did nothing to improve its ontological or epistemological soundness, it did improve its reliability. This is so since an assessment that takes into consideration the complex social, historical, and psychodynamic factors influencing a person's state of mind (*DSM-II*) is open to a greater range of interpretation than is the simple identification of symptoms that ignores those complexities. Both the *DSM-IV* and *DSM-5* are but a continuation and elaboration of the symptom-focused *DSM-III*.

Unfortunately for psychodiagnosis, attaining good reliability is based on having first established the validity of a diagnosis which can be found reliable, and on this more fundamental point, the *DSM* fails still more decisively. As Horwitz and Wakefield (2007) spell out in their thorough study, symptom-based criteria alone fail to produce valid diagnoses since psychological symptoms are always context-dependent. There are always contextual complexities, such as, age, sex, race, social, and economic factors, as well as physiological and environmental contingencies that call for a more nuanced, complex appraisal than the *DSM* permits. In their study of depression, they found that the *DSM-IV-TR* is unable to distinguish between depressive disorders and normal sorrow, since many, if not most, of the symptoms belonging to each are shared by both. This finding should be particularly disturbing to those who put their faith in "evidence-based" scientific findings, since a distinguishing feature of the *DSM-IV-TR* revision is that it is more empirically "evidence-based."

Horwitz and Wakefield observe that there are powerful vested interests motivated to perpetuate what has become an obfuscation of normal sadness into the mental disorder of depression. These interests include the juggernaut of the pharmaceutical industry, the academic research community funded by grants privileging empirical science, the American Medical and Psychiatric Associations, psychological service providers, a growing self-help market, the

National Alliance for the Mentally Ill, and perhaps most importantly, the public itself. The truth is that we, the people, do not want to suffer the inevitable confusions, anxieties, and despair that come with living a mortal life. Not to mention the exacerbated anxieties that come from living life within a materialistic and increasingly frantic techno-centric society suffering from the disintegration of the family, the community, the environment, and traditional religious institutions.

For instance, if a child is having "social problems" at school and home, cannot sustain attention on tasks or follow directions without getting distracted, is agitated and often irritating or downright aggressive, does he have an "Attention Deficit Disorder" such as ADHD, thus in need of medication and placement in "special" education? Or/and, is he over-stimulated and perhaps neurologically infected by the 24/7 anxiety-ridden fever of the furiously-paced, hyper-stimulating, and often impersonal culture he finds himself swept up in? Is it the individual child who is mentally "disordered?"

Or again, if I have lost a love of my life and feel hopeless and despairing because of that, sleeping long hours or suffering insomnia, feeling hopeless, unable to enjoy the life I once loved, and unsure whether I want to go on living at all, am I clinically depressed, thus in need of medication and perhaps cognitive-behavioral therapy to correct my irrational thoughts? Or, am I understandably grief-stricken, thus in need of supportive friends and family, time to mourn a wrenching loss and contemplate its meaning, perhaps with some existentially-robust therapy or spiritual guidance? This is a question of distinguishing a normal life transition from an abnormal mental disease: the basic task of pathology-discriminating diagnosis. Yet, the *DSM* is unable to validly and reliably make this discernment.

In basing psychodiagnosis strictly on an accounting of symptoms and thereby categorizing an individual as disordered, the *DSM* adheres to a basic principle of empirical science that requires the isolation of variables in order to arrive at objective truth, in this case a specific diagnosis. This is reductionistic. While reliability is improved by narrowing the focus to mere symptoms, validity is compromised. By failing to take the complexities of the environmental context into account, Horwitz and Wakefield argue that *DSM* diagnoses are invalid since they do not exist as they are posited, separate from the social and otherwise complex human context in which they arise. They conclude their study with the sweeping indictment that the *DSM-III/IV* revision is a failure, making a poor diagnostic manual substantially worse by blurring the distinctions between illness/disordered mental functioning and health/normal mental processes. Jacobs and Cohen (2009) come to the same conclusion from a slightly different perspective. Since *DSM* diagnoses presume to have scientific credibility ("evidence-based") when they lack any such validity, the *DSM* is a brash display of *pseudoscience*.

In addition to this research, the *Psychodynamic Diagnostic Manual (PDM)*, recently conceived as an alternative to the *DSM* for psychodynamically-oriented clinicians, cites further research studies. The editorial task force of the comprehensive *PDM* has handily compiled a collection of key research articles, including meta-analyses, citing additional studies which specifically discuss the reliability and validity problems of the *DSM* (*PDM* Task Force, 2006, Part III). The serious research diagnostician will profit by consulting these studies.

As devastating as Horwitz and Wakefield's analysis is to the credibility of the *DSM*, their work is aimed at its rehabilitation, and this agenda stalls their critique just at the point where it becomes relevant to human science and experiential therapies. And, while the *PDM* offers a viable alternative to the *DSM* that *does* take contextual factors into account, it does not go so far as to challenge the tacit assumptions of empirical psychodiagnosis. True to empiricism, in the *PDM* the researcher-diagnostician retains the privileged position of being (supposedly) an objective observer of a disjunct Other. To this extent at least, the *PDM* remains experience-distant. A more thorough critique could, and should, be rendered to the empirical assumptions which ground the *DSM* and, often unwittingly, many Psychoanalytic, Humanistic, and Transpersonal diagnostic schemas. Only by stepping outside of the objectivizing vision of empiricism and adopting a decidedly subjective/

inter-subjective approach to the knowing of Other minds, will the diagnostic theory serving experience-near therapies accord to their non-reductionistic, relational, and contextually-informed practices.

CHAPTER TWO

Revisioning Psychological Diagnosis

Not everything that can be counted counts, and not everything that counts can be counted.

—Albert Einstein

The Meaning of *dia-gnosis*

Due to its objectifying (thus dehumanizing) discourse, in which clusters of symptoms are reified into mental disorders and attributed to a discrete, personal self, the *DSM* misdirects practices of experientially-robust and holistically-oriented therapies. Although the *DSM* may be the most flagrantly objectivizing diagnostic system, privileging as it does the *content* of objective categories over the *process* of a living subjectivity, the tendency to assess others according to preconceived categories is not limited to the *DSM*. Humanistic, Transpersonal, and Integral diagnostic systems which are tacitly based on empirical scientific assumptions likewise posit delimited categories into which people are conformed. Categorical ways of thinking about others and encouraging them to think about themselves, clash with experience-near therapies which emphasize felt sensing, the search for authenticity, and thinking outside of boxes.

Yet, if we understand "diagnosis" in its originary sense, unconfined by its practice according to the priorities of the medical model, it is possible to diagnose with fidelity to core humanistic and transpersonal values that inform experientially-rigorous therapies. The word *diagnosis* is a combination of *gnosis*, which means to know, and *dia*, which means through or thorough. In its basic sense, *diagnosis* refers simply to a thorough knowing. In regard to other minds, what kind of knowing is it that grants the most thorough access? And, how thorough can this knowledge be? Echoing the meaning of *gnosis* in Christian mysticism and *prajna* in Buddhist psychology, this can be understood as a non-conceptual form of knowing.

Above all, experiential therapies attend to psychic and somatic subtleties in order to access the implicit complexities, inner contradictions, and unrealized potentialities that are often embedded in psychological depths. This requires a nuanced assessment in order to gauge therapeutic responses that more closely accord to the actuality of an Other's experience and to what the Other is ready and able to hear. Responses that are better keyed to a client's readiness to face difficult truths arise from a knowing that is more empathic than conceptual, more spontaneous than categorical, more intuitive than discursive. Attending to the immediacy of experience rather than conceptual constructs about experience, intuitive knowing is an appeal to a co-presence that is inclusive (*dia*) as well as direct (*gnosis*). So, how does one *diagnosis* another person in this holistic, experiential sense?

Toward a Contemplative Science of Diagnosis

There have been a number of constructive efforts to soften the pathological edge of objectivizing diagnoses in general and the *DSM* in particular. Several critiques (Hutchins, 2002; Ingersoll, 2002; Jerry, 2003; Lukoff, 1985 & 1988) have sought to minimize the *DSM*'s overtly pathologizing character by emphasizing positive characteristics and transpersonal potentialities of the human condition. However, as constructive as these and related revisions are, they continue to categorize others according to logical landscapes of objectively posited criteria, such as *DSM* v-codes, personality typologies, or discrete levels within a spectrum of consciousness. They remain expressions of a thinking which does not fully succeed in liberating the knowing of others from a discourse of reification, a *knowing about*, which posits an Other, and Otherness, as external to the conceiving subject. To this extent, they fall short of more radically holistic *trans*-personal and *inter*-subjective forms of understanding.

Psychodynamic, Humanistic, and Transpersonal diagnostics have not yet fully taken to heart the epistemological implications arising from the understanding that observed behavior does not exist apart from the observer of that behavior. To more fully comprehend the *inter-ness* of subjective experience, it is necessary to make a leap of cognition, from a conceptual to a contemplative—a non-conceptual, or trans-conceptual—kind of cognition. If one does not make this leap, this *trans-*, then one winds up thinking and talking about intersubjective and transpersonal experiences *as if* they were objective, self-existing realities. Among others, Jorge Ferrer (2002) and Peter Fenner (2002) describe how the emphasis on reifying and personalizing spiritual experience limits the development of transpersonal theory and the potentialities for *trans*personal realization.

It seems to me that the ontological and epistemological basis for a mature Transpersonal Psychology must be the recognition that human experience is quintessentially *trans-*, impermanent, a phenomenon of motility that cannot be captured within the notion of a Self (or Other) as a static, encapsulated entity. To maintain fidelity to *trans*personal experience and experientially-based therapies, selfhood is best understood as a *process* that is both *intersubjective*, embedded in and inseparable from the world of others and otherness, and *intentional*, a meaning-seeking project hurtling through a time that it co-creates. Rather than assuming the observer/observed split as the beginning of inquiry and proceeding on that basis, contemplative attention turns back on itself, folding the observer into the field of observation.

As difficult as it can be to make a discrimination between normal sadness and depression, for integral and holistically-oriented psychologies the diagnostic task is still more challenging. The question is not only that of making a discernment between pathological and non-pathological mental states, but holistically-oriented clinicians and clergy must also consider the maturational potential hidden within a "dark night of the soul." In addition to seeing loss as a normal part of mortal life, it is also possible to recognize that a wrenching loss may break one's heart open to deeper personal and interpersonal meaning and open a door to a more profound transpersonal presence. It seems to me that what we call *wisdom* is often a capacity born and bred in firestorms of psychic suffering in which we feel, and perhaps behave, not at all "normal" or emotionally "orderly." In fact, we may suffer, perhaps much longer than we, our family, and our doctor would like, from symptoms that perfectly describe the disease of depression. If this is the case, 1) should our "depression" be mitigated through medications so to ease our pain and return us to our "previous level of functioning," or 2) is it better that our "normal grief" be given a socially-circumscribed period of time to be experienced, after which time we are expected to "move on," or 3) should our "broken-openness" be deliberately cultivated (Chodron, 1997; Schneider, 2009; Taylor, 2009) so to increase our capacity for being open and embracing the mystery of life and death, perhaps finding a deeper humility, wisdom, and compassion to enjoy for ourselves and to share with others? Or, should these "ors" 1), 2), and 3), also be considered as "ands"? In order to make this kind of discernment it is necessary to allow for a far more inclusive approach than that permitted by empiricism.

An alternative view that recognizes the subject matter of psychology to be of the nature of human subjectivity must be based on wholly different grounds than that of empirical materialism. It is not that the scientific method and the knowledge it generates needs to be rejected out of hand, but that this view and its knowledge be subordinated to a broader holistic orientation.

Since empiricism has dictated the epistemological terms of diagnostic formulation, it is necessary to reassess those terms in framing an alternative approach. Whereas ontology addresses the nature of human subjectivity, the *who* who is being understood, epistemology details *how* that understanding comes about. *How* one approaches, and sees, another person influences to a considerable degree *what* knowledge is relevant to know about that person. The principal challenge in any form of psychodiagnosis is to see the Other as accurately as possible as they are, undistorted by the diagnostician's personal or professional projections.

Holistic reorientation requires a double shift in terms of how we consider human subjectivity (*being*) and time. In terms of subjectivity, it requires a contemplative shift from thinking conceptually *about* others as self-existing, empirically observable entities (who can then be inserted into preconceived categories) to an emphasis on felt experiencing that is intersubjective in the sense that it thinks *with* otherness. It also requires, as Husserl (1964/1928) noted, a shift in conceiving of time as something that exists objectively and is external to the experiencer, like a river one is passively floating on, to a recognition that time is a subjective experience, internal to a consciousness engaged in the passing moment and whose passage does not occur apart from one's participation in the moment. This shifts the focus from what *has* happened or what *might yet* happen to a focus on what *is* happening just now within and between us. This does not mean that we attend to the present moment to the exclusion of the past or future, but that we notice—when something arises to notice—how the momentum of the past may be construing a future through our (perhaps unwitting) participation in it.

As mentioned above, phenomenology is a particularly rigorous approach that has taken this daunting challenge to heart, so it makes sense to draw upon this intellectually robust and research-seasoned tradition. (For instance, Boss, 1982/1963; Gendlin 1973a & 1973b; Giorgi, 1985; Husserl, 1970/1954; Kruger, 1979: Luijpen, 1960; Merleau-Ponty,

1963/1942 & 1962; and Spinelli, 1989.)

In seeing an individual, couple, family, or any social grouping, as a *phenomenon* rather than as an entity existing in an external object world disjunct from an internal observer, phenomenology and related experiential methods recognize that a relationship of mutual influence exists between self and other, self and world. A "phenomenon" is simply "that which reveals itself." Thinking in terms of *phenomena*, the harsh dualistic vision of empiricism is considerably softened, preparing the way for holistic understanding. This approach respects and preserves the mystery of existence in general and subjectivity in particular. It invites the Other to reveal her or himself as they are, as free as possible from the reducing lens of the observer's biases, and remains open to take into account various contextual and psychological complexities.

General Criteria for Revisioning Diagnosis

This section identifies a few critical shifts that characterize the epistemological transition from an empirical to a holistic approach which can serve as criteria for the development of alternative diagnostic approaches. This list gathers together guidelines proposed from many quarters over the past century.

From content-based to process-based psychology

In regard to ontology—drawing upon the thought of Existential-Phenomenology and Buddhist psychology— *human nature, the basic subject matter of psychology, is seen to be fundamentally free.* Subjectivity is fundamentally motile, malleable, and unconditioned. Human nature is such that we are free to become stuck, to get unstuck, or to remain open, to be conditioned or unconditioned, reactive or reasonable, constrained or spontaneous, dignified and individuated, or to find ourselves (as B. F. Skinner (1971) found us) beyond freedom and dignity. Human consciousness exists not in a fixed, detached mind, but in a river of time wherein we are free to live the same year in the same way over and over or to live each day anew. The inherent freedom of human *being* calls for a *process-based* psychology, in which the more accurate understanding of a person sees that person as an on-going work-in-progress. This does not mean a person is destined to change an old habit, but that a person *might* change.

Knowledge of an Other would thus recognize the Other as a being that is more like a verb than a noun. In contrast, empiricist ontology is content-based. It conceives of Others nominatively, as self-contained entities. This recognition suggests that holding to any fixed diagnostic categorization is in a basic sense flawed. It is thus more appropriate to think diagnostically in dynamic terms such as habits, practices, and tendencies, rather than in static terms such as states, types, or other nominative categories.

From prediction and control to spontaneity and freedom

Several critical epistemological distinctions can be made between empiricism and holism. Perhaps most importantly, the prime directive of empirical science is to enable the "prediction and control" of nature, thus necessitating a decisive separation between man and nature, self and world, mind and body, et cetera. On the other hand, *the prime directive of holistic psychologies is to enable a person's capacity to be fully human*. While "fully human" may be understood in various ways, here it refers to the capacity to be more completely present in the world. Full presence involves the capability of being both *open* and *responsive* to others, the world, and oneself. Instead of valuing prediction and control of nature, holistic psychologies value the freedom of spontaneity and the deepening of trust in the openness and at times *un*predictable responsiveness of human interaction. Again, the point is not that self-control or the making of reasoned predictions are rejected, but it is recognized that they arise from and remain rooted in a broader holistic context and capacity for being present. Within this understanding, mental health professionals are challenged to discriminate between genuine openness and spontaneous responsiveness and contrived presence, reactivity, and defensiveness.

From objectivity to intersubjectivity

While empiricism begins by making a sharp separation between the observed object and the observing of that object, privileging the objectivity of the observer, a holistic approach begins by allowing connections to emerge between observer and observed, privileging the intersubjectivity of the encounter. Intersubjectivity is here understood in two senses. In the common sense, it refers to the contextual recognition that a therapeutic or psychological assessment situation is always an interaction between (at least) two subjectivities, each of which bring their respective life experiences and independent unconscious organizing principles to bear on the exchange (Stolorow & Atwood, 1992). With this understanding, the therapist no longer assumes himself to be a neutral, detached observer who exercises little or no influence on his client. Instead, the therapist is enjoined to take into account both what he sees in the other person and how he himself is being impacted by that person, which may be shaping (perhaps unconsciously) what he sees or fails to see.

In a second, more subtle sense, intersubjectivity recognizes the *field*, or *inter-ness*, within which distinct subjectivities interact (Bradford, 2007). The *place* of an interpersonal exchange is the in-between space, or as Winnicott (1971) referred to it, "potential space," that is essential to any exchange even as it is indefinable. Allowing for the inter-ness of subjectivity opens the way for a therapist or spiritual guide and client or spiritual seeker to respect, and perhaps rest in, the unconditioned presence of human experience. Granted, consideration of the ontological freedom of an intersubjective attunement which can allow for the emergence of mystery, awe, and unconditional openness, may have limited application in much psychology and therapy, still, for those compelled, or graced, to seek deeper truth, this understanding opens a door that is most relevant. (Prendergast & Bradford, 2007; Schneider, 2004 & 2009; Welwood, 2000)

From de-contextualized to context-based assessment

The scientific method is based on isolating, or de-contextualizing, variables in order to test a specific hypothesis. This is done in order to eliminate extraneous variables that might interfere with determining the significance of the specific variable being researched. On the other hand, a human scientific approach seeks to comprehend the totality of a person within their life situation. The assumption here is not that a person exists as an isolatable mind, but that one is always a *being in the world*, inextricable from the social and natural contexts in which he or she is embedded. This approach reverses the empiricist mandate by requiring the *inclusion of variables* in any viable psychological assessment. In addition to the various dimensions of the social context which should be considered, such as culture, family, race, age, sex, and a range of socio-economic factors, it may also be relevant to consider still other contextual influences. These might include such factors as the climate and season, geography, physical condition, dietary practices, and spiritual propensities.

From logical deduction to intuition and empathic understanding

The prime cognitive function which empiricism exercises in determining scientific truth is logical deduction. Holistically-informed science certainly respects the exercise of logic, deductive and inductive, but also calls for a significantly wider exercise of cognizance. Phenomenology explicitly privileges the exercise of *intuition* as the cognitive function most able to comprehend the implicit complexities of human experience (Gurwitsch,1964/1957; Husserl, 1962/1913). Intuition functions as an inclusive form of knowing by taking into consideration the contextual breadth and depth of a phenomenon, allowing unfettered reach and range to inquisitive awareness. Understandings that emerge intuitively are more able to reveal the holistic structure of a situated human experience and are more in accord with the nature of experience as being in-process. Empathic attunement is an akin mode of cognition that functions according to and within an interpersonal field.

Empathy is distinguished from intuition in being a more stridently feeling-keyed knowing. More importantly, these forms of cognizance are akin in that they are *non-conceptual* (or *pre-conceptual* or *trans-conceptual*) forms of cognition. While conceptual logic excels as a nominative function, dividing a whole into parts and distinguishing between those parts, intuition and empathy excel in comprehending a sense of whole experiences, including the dynamic inter-relations between parts. The key assumption here is that the whole person is always more than the sum of her parts, will always elude conceptual understanding, and that to know a person more completely it is necessary to "think" with ones heart as much as one's mind.

From impersonal causality to a participatory subject

Within the empiricist worldview, subjectivity—including personality structure and interpersonal relationship—is seen as a result of impersonal causes. As Boss (1983, Chapter 12) notes, by focusing primarily on past preconditions of a current problematic situation, the causal approach relegates the human subject to a passive status. As a mere effect of predefining causes, a personal condition is thus defined as an impersonal artifact. Within this mindset, psychological problems readily lend themselves to being conceived by physiological causes such as faulty neurotransmitters or biochemical imbalances, or as resulting from social or psychological causes, such as deficient or traumatic parenting or other social forces. Of course, the manifold and compelling conditions of life exert tremendous formative influence on human subjectivity. *But influence is not the same as impersonal causality.*

A human subject is always involved in *personally responding* to the life conditions in which she finds herself. The assumption of individual response-ability is a cornerstone for the rule of law, democracy, and the work of psychotherapy. However, empiricist causal thinking does not, and cannot, account for this basic freedom. As Jacobs and Cohen (2009) observe, "The *DSM's* pathology framework…is about what happens to people based on impersonal processes and mechanisms; it does not address the person's situation as far as he or she is concerned." (p.317). From a human science perspective, a person's *concern* for his situation, his *participation* in it, is what really matters. Psychotherapy works, when it does work, because we accept that it is less important *what* happened to us than *how* we took, and continue to take, what happened to us. It is by recognizing our participation in the life we are currently living that we have a chance of changing it going forward. On this pivot turns the effectiveness of any self-reflection, psychotherapy, or spiritual awakening.

Concluding Thoughts

While there are expedient reasons to continue to profes-
sionally reference the *DSM*, such as for insurance reim-
bursement or to communicate with medical personnel,
issues of expediency ought not be confounded with scientific issues of validity and reliability. On scientific, clinical,
and ethical grounds, the *DSM* fails as a valid diagnostic
instrument. Given its prominence in the mental health
field, this failure needs to be highlighted both in clinical
training situations and in everyday clinical practice. In the
course of such expose, the assumptions of empirical science which inform the *DSM* must also be brought into
question. Complementing critiques of empiricism and the
DSM, alternative diagnostic approaches and formulae need
to be developed according to specifically human scientific
guidelines. Among the guidelines that can be identified,
holistically-oriented science asserts that the purpose of a
psychological diagnosis is to enhance the spontaneity and
freedom of a human subject, that it be contextualized and
inclusive of variables, privileging intuition and empathic
understanding as prime cognizant functions, and see the
person(s) being diagnosed as a participatory subject, a free
and responsible agent. Additionally, an accurate knowing
of Other minds must be process-based, recognizing that
a human subject is not a detached, isolated mind but a
being that exists within an intersubjective field, including

a diagnostic field that is co-constituted by both doctor and patient.

CHAPTER THREE

Mindfulness-Based Assessment and Diagnosis

If our science of mental health is to become more effective, psychotherapists will have to balance their knowledge of psychological concepts and techniques with a contemplative awareness...that exercises itself day after day in quiet openness.

—Medard Boss

From the Buddhist point of view, there is a problem with any attempt to pinpoint, categorize, and pigeonhole mind and its contents very neatly. This method could be called psychological materialism. The problem with this approach is that it does not leave enough room for spontaneity or openness. It overlooks basic healthiness.

—Chogyam Trungpa

Recognizing that the intersubjective field is the actual locus in which any psychological diagnosis is made, as clinicians we can acknowledge straight away that in "my" getting to

know "you," your "youness" is mediated through my seeing of you and all the influences that form the contours
of my vision. Thus, a fundamental question for diagnosis
becomes: Is it possible for me to see you as you are or only
as I conjure you through my personal projections and theoretical constructs? To the extent that I see you as I conjure
you, who is it I am actually diagnosing? To the extent I see
you as you are, how is it that I am able to do this?

Following Heidegger's rough distinction between
"calculative thinking" and "meditative thinking," we will
consider the first question through an examination of discursive thinking and empirically-informed diagnosis, and
the latter question through a consideration of meditative
thinking and phenomenological inquiry. In so doing, we
will explore how psychological knowing can proceed as a
mindfulness practice of *interpersonal meditation*.

Contemplative diagnosis as discussed here is offered to
serve psychotherapies and psychospiritual disciplines which
seek to facilitate existential reckoning and transpersonal
awakening. This approach may not be necessary for therapies and spiritual direction which have more modest goals.

Calculative Thinking and Empirical Assessment

The mind strives to make sense of things. It forms *gestalts*,
imposing an order on the apparent chaos of experience.
We are compelled to wrap the immensity of *being* into a

coherent picture, into constructs within which we feel oriented and secure. In this way we construct an inhabitable world, create "myths to live by" that give meaning and purpose to our lives and the lives of others. However, the orientation and mastery we thereby gain comes at a price. We become captivated within our intentional thought processes and live inside boxes in which we do not recognize, or tend to forget, that it is our own calculating minds that have constructed a self-limited, provisional world. Calculative thought is at constant risk of taking its relative constructs, including diagnostic formulations, as absolute givens, and losing itself in the process.

As Heidegger put it, "Calculative thinking computes.... [It] races from one prospect to the next...never stops, never collects itself" (1966/1959, p.46). Moving from project to project, concept to concept, the calculating mind always looks outward. Thus, we remain hidden to ourselves. Self-hiddeness and the processes of projection it begets give rise to experience that is chronically anxious and incomplete. Whether in our personal lives or in working with others, calculating mind feels itself lacking something, which can give rise to an urgency to fill the sense of inner lack with some outer thing, experience, or knowledge (Loy, 1996). All the while we are perpetuating the split between self and other/world, but without awareness that we are doing so. Psychodiagnosis inadvertently reinforces this estrangement when it succumbs to the anxiety of the striving mind—including the wanting-to-help mind—and focuses solely on the pursuit of something out there and then rather than here and now.

In terms of psychotherapy, how much favor do we wish to grant calculative thinking and the influence such thought is likely to have over our clients and our therapy? As Germer, Seigel, & Fulton (2005) put it,

> Problems arise when we take our descriptive clinical categories to be natural representations of an objective world of disorders, conveniently provided in a treatment manual....A diagnostic label used as a kind of shorthand can come to replace a more nuanced appraisal of the whole person. In the process, we stop looking, convinced that we know enough. It becomes a cover for our ignorance, masquerading as knowledge and certainty. (p.69)

Calculative thought tends to reify opinions and ideas which it then clings to as armor against the inherently unsettled, impermanent nature of existence. The positing of objective diagnoses, including personality typologies, may be just another way of defending ourselves—as therapists and clients alike—against the unpredictability of life by imposing a schematic order upon it. To the extent we cling to a reified view of Self and Other, regardless of the reference system defining those categories, we introduce fixation into the exchange.

> To hold any fixed view, including a fixed view of
> our patients or ourselves, leads to suffering. Fixed
> positions are snapshots, arrested moments sam-
> pled from an unfolding flux, instantly out of date.
> The desire to find something stable is natural; we
> seek certainty to bind the anxiety of the unknown.
> Once we take up a position, we begin to defend it
> and attempt to shape our view of reality to fit our
> concepts. (p.71)

Unwilling to tolerate the anxiety and tensions within transient experiencing, we latch onto a fixed view of the Other, thus partitioning them and distancing ourselves from them. This may temporarily reduce our anxiety, but only by risking a solidification of the relational field between us. A calculating mindset is keyed to ignoring its own subjectivity by focusing on identifying, labeling, and categorizing an Other (even if that other is oneself).

The psychological impact psychodiagnosis can have on a client, quite apart from the diagnostic value it may hold for a clinician, will be exemplified in the following vignettes of a client I will call Beatrice. Her story is per-tinent in that she was diagnosed both empirically and contemplatively.

The Story of Beatrice, Take 1:
Conventional Empirical Diagnosis

In her early twenties, Beatrice began suffering bouts of terror which would briefly incapacitate her. She had grown up in a family culture of withering criticism and bruising disavowal, especially from her mother, who would occasionally tell Bea that she wished she would never have been born. In college, Bea consulted a counselor who referred her to a psychiatrist who diagnosed her as having a panic disorder coupled with a clinical depression. Medication was prescribed and short-term counseling attempted, but these were of little help. In fact, Bea wound up regretting reaching out for help, since the diagnosis of her pathology seemed to confirm her mother's accusations that she was fundamentally flawed. Only this time it was a credible medical authority who indicted her. Beatrice carried this assessment of herself as a shameful weight for the next twenty years. Through various psychological consultations and her own research during this period, she discovered some behavioral techniques for managing the panic attacks and was able to get by. "Getting by" meant living in fear of being incapacitated by an anxiety attack at any moment. Although she sensed there might be some meaning to her anxiety, something that was not merely a confirmation of her disorderedness, she was afraid of opening herself to a psychologist for fear of again being pathologized.

Beatrice Take 2:
Transpersonal-Empirical Diagnosis

While stretching conventional psychology to include spiritual potentials, transpersonal thought has not yet thoroughly challenged the dualistic assumptions of empirical science (Ferrer, 2002). Accepting the empiricist principles of the *DSM* and working within that context, Transpersonal theorists such as Lukoff, Lu & Turner (1998) and Jerry (2003) are working to revise the *DSM* to include "religious and spiritual problems" as v-codes. Others, such as Hutchins (2002) and Ingersoll (2002), are working to complement the standard differential diagnosis of the *DSM* by envisioning axes that include alternative and/ or non-pathological criteria. Sympathetic to the principles of "positive psychology," Hutchins proposes a 5 axis "gnosis model," which complements the pathologically-skewed *DSM* with an assessment of gifts, callings, and abilities. While Ingersoll, who accepts *DSM* diagnoses as a "necessary evil," complements this with a broader "integral differential diagnosis" based on Ken Wilber's work. In addition to providing refreshing alternatives to the *DSM*, these kinds of diagnostic calculi deserve no small merit insofar as they authorize a focus on humanistic and transpersonal potentialities and are valuable in reducing anxiety and despair by helping to mitigate negative self-assessments.

For instance, identifying my fixation point on the

Enneagram may lessen the anxiety and self-criticism I feel as I realize that I am not a mutant, but belong to whole class of kindred spirits who are similarly fixated. This knowledge may well allow me to be more self-accepting. In addition, once I Ennea-type you and see that the disturbing way in which you relate to me is less about me than about your own fixation style, I may be able to take your "attitude" less personally, be more understanding and forgiving. Nevertheless, *let us not mistake a calculative project that helps us get along better in samsara with a contemplative undertaking which aims at freeing us from samsara.*[1] *It seems to me that any genuine transpersonal psychology ought not take its eye off this big freedom.*

It is important to respect that Transpersonal Psychology is a "big tent" discipline, making space for myriad spiritual and psychological approaches. The particular understanding of "*trans*-personal" I am sketching is but one of several understandings. In fact, no fewer than forty definitions of transpersonal psychology have been catalogued (Lajoie & Shapiro, 1992). While a contemplative approach recognizing the nondual nature of existence and aiming toward awakening from *samsara* is surely within the Transpersonal field, it does not follow that all Transpersonal approaches are "contemplative" in this sense. Much transpersonally-inspired psychology remains empirically and dualistically informed, as Bea discovered.

During the years following her initial diagnosis,

Beatrice was a student of spirituality and occasional Zen practitioner, and at the end of this period found the courage to seek guidance from a popular psychospiritual organization that included individual sessions and group process as part of a comprehensive program of psychospiritual development. Although the individual and group sessions were often conducted by licensed therapists who were themselves advanced students in the program, the organization was careful to distinguish what it did as "education" rather than "psychotherapy," and screened new students to ascertain their readiness to engage in what could be evocative and psychologically challenging work. To assess a student's readiness, program counselors rely heavily on psychoanalytic developmental theory. This is ostensibly done for the sake of the student, to make sure he or she has enough "ego strength" to handle the rigors of indepth experiential work.

As with other such programs, the screening process is based on the conventional assumption that there is an observable and valid difference between psychopathology (including weak ego strength) and spiritual readiness (strong ego strength). The thing is: How do you accurately assess ego strength? If we are honest about it, this is a measure which turns out to be impossible to objectively ascertain. Where does an "ego" appear which can be identified much less measured as to its relative strength? In adopting an empiricist frame of reference to assess its students, even an unabashedly transpersonal program resorts to an objectivizing, if not pseudoscientific, form of assessment, which pollutes the nondual orientation according to which its holistic program is presumably based.

In Beatrice's case, following a nearly year-long screening period while awaiting the start of new training group, it was decided that she was not a candidate for the deep work the program offered. Her individual teacher/counselor decided that she lacked readiness due to her ongoing anxieties and potential of having further panic attacks, as well as her inability to develop a sufficiently "trusting relationship" with the counselor. Although a few of her positive qualities were reflected back to her, Bea was rejected from the program and advised to seek remedial psychotherapy to address her unreadiness for "deeper work." This second diagnosis and the rejection it occasioned hit Bea quite hard, confirming once again that she was seriously flawed, this time not by a cruel mother or a random psychiatrist, but by a spiritual authority whose judgment she respected. Worse, this diagnosis felt still more entrapping than the earlier one, since at this point she was in midlife and more aware that her time was limited. Her anxiety, hopelessness, and desperation escalated. It was at this point that she sought me out.

Meditative Thinking and
Phenomenological Assessment

Heidegger describes meditative thinking as "openness to the mystery," in which our normal habit of dualistic thinking is loosened, allowing unmediated awareness (*gnosis, prajna*) to function spontaneously. The meditative openness of which Heidegger speaks is informed by a phenomenological epistemology and method of inquiry. To see another person as a phenomenon, or mystery, is both to invite the Other to reveal herself as she is and to be willing to be awe-struck by her Otherness. Adapted to clinical inquiry, phenomenology can serve as a bridge between calculative thinking and contemplative knowing.

Within calculative thought, psychological reference systems mediate experience through the conceptual lens of their theories. Depending on the priorities of the system, some elements of experience come into sharper focus while other elements remain fuzzy or are ignored. Without rejecting the value that may come from seeing the Other through the lens of any particular system or through multiple lenses of several systems (as in Integral approaches), phenomenology endeavors to encounter others as they reveal (and conceal) themselves, as free as possible from the mediating concepts of any reference system.

Phenomenological inquiry proceeds by intentionally "bracketing" the filtering constructs of the therapist's reference systems in order to discover how the client is tacitly constructing his own self-world. This method presents us with the paradoxical challenge of meditative attention, which, as Heidegger observed, "At times requires a greater effort. It demands more practice. It is in need of even more delicate care than any other genuine craft. But it must also be able to bide its time, to await as does the farmer, whether the seed will come up and ripen" (1959/1966, p.47).

Within calculative thought, diagnosis is an orienting function conducted prior to a treatment function which is based upon it. But for experientially-based meditative awareness, the separation between these functions does not hold, as diagnosis is already part of the treatment. In getting to know a person, the way in which we approach the Other is already making an impression on that person. In diagnosing someone, we are already "treating" the person in a particular way and with a particular attitude, which may, for instance, encourage or discourage the person's trust and self-disclosure, as it did for Beatrice.

Since we can only gain access to an Other's mind through participating with that mind, phenomenological knowing requires from the outset that we take into consideration how we are seeing, and perhaps distorting, the Other through our own constructs. In order to minimize distortion and open our field of vision, it is of primary importance to bracket any assumptions of belief or disbelief we have in regard to the Other and what he has to say.

The therapist neither confirms nor disconfirms the truth of a person's story, but is challenged to listen as unconditionally as possible, with what Freud called "evenly-suspended attention." This is similar to the mindfulness practice of *bare attention*: moment to moment sensory awareness.[2] Whereas our usual tendency is to get caught up in calculative thoughts and react emotionally in regard to them, meditative attention temporarily suspends the striving of discursive thinking. Without trying to keep anything in mind or to push anything away, the therapist can more readily enter into the intersubjective field, allowing for increasingly subtle and complex perceptions to arise.

As Heidegger notes, "Meditative thinking demands of us not to cling one-sidedly to a single idea, nor to run down a one-track course of ideas. Meditative thinking demands of us that we engage ourselves with what at first sight does not go together at all" (p.53). This invites us to attune to the "felt sense" (Gendlin, 1978) that opens to the totality of an experience, even though we may not be able to say what that totality is. Effectively, this practice is a rudimentary form of interpersonal meditation, and as such is a unique contribution of Western psychology to traditional Eastern solo meditation practices.

Beatrice Take 3:
Phenomenological-Contemplative Diagnosis

Being present within the felt saturation of an intersubjective field, knowledge arises intuitively and empathically
through explicating what is implicit within that field. For
example, when Bea told me how her mother ruthlessly
belittled her as a child, I was less drawn to what happened
to her than with how she took, and continues to take, what
happened to her (this being what was happening as we
spoke). In our conversations, she spoke of what struck me
as horrible experiences with a wan smile. But the smile did
not correspond to the humiliation I was empathically feeling in listening to her story. Being moved by the tragedy,
yet without either validating her as being a victim or invalidating the gravity of what happened, I was able to observe
what I felt as the incongruity of her smile in conjunction
with the horror I was sensing in what she was saying. As
I shared this observation with her, she blanched, paused,
looked me in the eye, and said in a shaky voice, "I know.
That nervous smile. I think I do that alot." In this exchange,
I described something that was still largely implicit for her,
and for me. Yet my reflection did not rise to the level of an
objective diagnosis or even an interpretation, since I did
not grant it any meaning beyond the transient exchange we
were having. However, that Bea noticed this incongruity
as a habitual reaction on her part did mean something to

her, and potentially it could mean that she was flawed and could be taken as yet another proof of her unworthiness.

Bea's emotional incongruity reveals something of her *self and world construct* system (Bugental, 1978). Identifying a self-structure is a typical purpose of psychodiagnosis, including one phenomenologically-derived. It is not sufficient in phenomenology to describe various elements of subjective experience without intuiting the coherence of those elements. Phenomenological knowing seeks to comprehend how the various dimensions, inner tensions, contradictions, and potentialities of a person coalesce into an *invariant organization,* or *structure*, of subjectivity. As Idhe writes, the phenomenological method *"Seek[s] out structural or invariant features of the phenomena"* (1977, p.39). For phenomenology, there is no problem considering the informative constructs of multiple reference systems. Since the constructs of any reference system are to be bracketed within a meditative attention, one is less tempted to cling to the knowledge they delimit. Indeed, the formulations of some particular reference system(s) might fruitfully illuminate something of the Other's self-organization. However, such a formulation is to arise intuitively out of a meditative involvement with the Other rather than logically in deference to a preferred theory.

Even so, this more open, intuitive understanding of an Other's self-structure tends toward a subtle reification of that person. In seeking to discover "structural and invariant features," phenomenology presumes to arrive at a knowledge that is not conditioned by its method of questioning. In presuming to know an Other apart from the Self doing the knowing, phenomenology is emboldened to make a claim of absolute (invariant) knowledge. In so doing, meditative awareness is at risk of reverting to a form of calculative thinking.

In addition, as helpful as it is, the meditative method of evenly suspending judgment is an intentional act of holding biases and distractions at bay. This holding-back introduces a subtle separation into the inquiry. Awareness of the Other is still being managed from a distance, thus it is not fully *inter*-subjective and true to the transient nature of experience.

Identifying a structure of subjectivity does not reveal **who** *a person is. It reveals* **how** *a person is construing their world and the self they are taking themselves to be.* A self-world structure is a composition of psychological tendencies which are intentional (even if unconscious) practices one tends to repeat and so perpetuate. For experiential therapies, it is not enough to identify a self (-world) organizing structure, since merely identifying a fixation is rarely enough to release it. Remaining on a conceptual level does not penetrate the depths of conditioning. To more thoroughly liberate a construct of subjectivity, it is necessary to open to *how* one is intending (constructing) that self-world in order to not intend (construe) it into the future. The challenge is to experientially discover that one's (constructed) Self is not something (someone) one *is*, but is something (someone) one *practices*. Recognizing how I am (and have been) unconsciously participating in a particular, habitual way of being in the world opens the door for me to release that (structuring) participation. A more thorough self-liberation requires that I see—experience— that the Self is not an entity but a set of practices, a kind of play that I have been—and still am—unwittingly performing. Experientially-keyed therapy focuses attention on the moment-to-moment participation of how one is engaged in construing a self-world. Such attention is meditative in that it attends to what is ordinarily outside of conscious, calculating awareness. Being pre-reflective and non-conceptual, mindful awareness is thus more conducive to a wide range of empathic, energetic, somatic, and intuitive forms of cognizance.

Of course, it is also possible, and at times desirable, to proceed from pre-reflective openness to conceptual reflection and understanding. But we ought not lose sight that moving into self-reflection and conceptual discourse may shift the therapeutic exchange from a meditative to a calculative, perhaps reifying mindset. Certainly, there are many instances where moving from unintegrated feeling states into more conceptually-bounded states is called for. This is especially true when a person is at risk of being swamped by overwhelming affect which may trigger a retraumatization of some kind. But stepping back into conceptual reflection also makes sense as one strives to better understand one's hidden motives and unconscious reactions. The challenge for the experiential therapist is to move back and forth between unintegrated states, including unconstructed openness, and constructive understandings without reifying those constructions by lending the weight of professional authority to them.

In psychological knowledge, it is all too easy to think or speak about an insight into self or other as if that insight were something that exists in reality rather than as that which it is, as something that exists only in a conception of reality. For instance, it would be easy to speak of Bea's "critical superego," "negative maternal introject," or "inner critic," as if the critic, introject, or superego existed independent of our construction, and her practice, of it. Of course, naming this kind of thing is often a vital step toward releasing it, but only if it remains a step and is not formed into an identity.

While Bea did take her insight as yet another indictment against herself, I was struck by the *conviction* of her self-indictment, and said so. This gave her another pause. In this pause, Bea did not know what to think, and neither did I. For my part, practicing the best I could within a meditative awareness, I let myself relax in her presence without knowing what to say and without succumbing to the impulse to fill in this gap and relieve us of having to bear it. Shortly, while remaining silently attuned to her, I sensed Bea's mind starting to cogitate again and I wondered what she was experiencing. So I ventured, "What do you notice as we sit here?" This opened an exchange during which she oscillated between affirming the old self-construct of being flawed and that of opening to the possibility—which she experienced as "groundless"—that this might not be the case. This therapeutic traverse was nothing short of an identity crisis for her. If she was not fundamentally flawed, then fundamentally, who was she? In the oscillating play of this inquiry, each of us describing what we were noticing and noticing what we were describing, Bea and I were practicing an experience-near *explication* of meaning.

Explication Versus Interpretation

Whereas an *interpretation* makes meaning based on the concepts of a reference system that filter and funnel raw experience into particular constructs, an *explication* arises within the field of intersubjective experiencing and does not disengage from the felt complexity of that field (as does an interpretation). The meaning that arises through a process of explication is unique and unpredictable, unlike the calculated meanings that are interpreted according to preconceived categories within a particular theoretical system. Interpretations are content-based and serve utilitarian goals of expedience, proceeding in a single direction from chaos to order, from raw experience to conceptual understanding, from unconsciousness to consciousness.

On the other hand, explications arising through meditative attunement are process-based, and serve the sense of wonder. As Gendlin (1973) has discussed, meaningful understanding remains transitory and proceeds dialectically, oscillating between the implicit mysteries of felt experience and the explicit understandings which emerge from it. *In contemplative cognizance, diagnosis is no-thing.* It is neither the conceptual understanding, such as would be carried in words like "depression" or "incongruent," nor is it the mute, raw experience to which the words refer. Rather, diagnosis takes place in the to-and-fro between experience being understood and understanding being experienced, checked as to its felt accuracy, and then either released (if accurate) or re-understood (more accurately). True to the transient nature of experience, the process of explication aims not to "nail down" a meaning, but to "free up" meaningfulness by allowing for the emergence of deepening understandings. Since there is no end of experience, there is no end to the meaning we may discover through inquiring into it.

It turns out to be impossible, as Gendlin observes, to arrive at any invariant structure of subjectivity or any final meaning regarding who or what or how one is. Experience being endlessly variable, understanding is also endlessly variable. Facing the way things actually are reveals there is no fixed psychological structure, or ground, to be found, as Beatrice noticed in her brief but exhilarating experience of "groundlessness." For some moments, she found no constructs, and in those open, free-floating moments, there was no panic or anxiety, but an unfamiliar peace of mind. Her open-ended experience closed rather soon as worrisome thoughts started up again, but the gap of those moments left an impression. We noticed together that when she let herself be, groundlessness need not be feared; on the contrary, it offers a fertile avenue of experiencing she had not previously permitted.

Beatrice Take 4: Contemplative Diagnosing

Bea's initial guardedness, porcelain smile, and the shakiness of her voice revealed why her previous counselor may have concluded she was too brittle for indepth work. In the early weeks of our work, I too felt uncomfortable in her nervous presence. Yet I could also sense in her shaky voice, speaking as it did at times with direct eye contact, a fount of relational courage and self-honesty. For awhile, I did not know how to address this, and rather than force something, I decided to linger in the silence of my unknowing. Very soon, she revealed that she experienced my silence as terrifying, in the sense that she was populating it with her own fears that I might be judging her critically. Yet, she found the nerve to ask me about this, which facilitated my responding to her in a way that observed both her fear and her courage in daring to open and speak candidly about herself. Repeated exchanges like this led her to feel a "steadiness" with me, and so with herself, allowing her to take in that she could be *both* terrified *and* brave. She eventually disclosed that it was my simply being with her, more than any particular sense I made during that time, that allowed her to relax and trust both me and herself.

From a calculative perspective, Bea's previous counselor and I would probably have agreed on her psychodynamic diagnosis. However, we came to exactly opposite conclusions regarding what that meant for her readiness to engage in challenging depth work. I found Bea to have enough courage, candor, and capacity for relational openness required for such work. The crux of the difference was less *what* we each saw in Bea, since we saw some of the same things, than *how* we each saw her. Whereas a contemplative approach accents the *how* of the *what*, a calculative approach emphasizes the *what* over the *how*, privileging content over process.

Within a predominantly calculative attitude, the program counselor saw and reflected Bea back to herself as an anxious and rather difficult person with whom to relate. Seeing herself through the eyes of a scrutinizing Other and lacking the strength to shake off this gaze, Bea displayed herself as the object she was (yet again) being seen to be. Thus she confirmed the counselor's (and her own) vision of her as psychologically deficient. Caught in a dualistic vision, the counselor was not able to see the whole picture of what was happening. She did not see that it was not Bea, in herself, who was anxious and difficult to connect with, but that it was Bea *in relation to* the counselor that evoked anxiety. The difficulty did not lie solely with Bea and the intrapsychic dynamics of her separate mind, as Object Relations theory (which mediated the counselor's vision) affirms, but lay *between* the two of them. *Bea was experienced as difficult* for the counselor, but *the counselor's difficulty* was left out of the equation.

In contrast, by adopting a contemplative attitude, I was more able to remain aware of the subjective tensions that were influencing my own seeing as well as the tensions I was noticing in Beatrice. Remaining within the intersubjective field, I allowed that Bea's anxieties were not fixed inside her separate mind, but existed in the inter-ness, or *interbeing*,[3] between us. Within this less-divided vision, I did not assume that the relational problem belonged to either Bea or to me alone, but was in an experiential sense *ours*. The sense of relatedness Bea felt in this approach allowed her to relax her guard, and with the immediacy of the relational contact permitting little room for distraction, pressed her to open herself and to be seen/see herself as she was in relationship rather than in isolation. Thus, I believe I came to see potentialities in Bea her previous counselor missed.

While it is true that I did not have to screen Bea for

admission to a psychospiritual program, I did need to screen her as a psychotherapy client whom I could treat within the scope of my competence. Since an Other can only be known, and treated, through My knowing and treating of her, it makes no sense to screen the readiness of a supposedly isolated "I," but only the *compatibility* of the other person and me (or the program I represent). It was unfortunate for Bea that she was identified as inadequate in herself, when the truth was that the inadequacy was in the incompatibility between her and the skillful means at the disposal of the program. It would have been both more honest and more humble for the program's counselor to have admitted that she herself was unable to establish a good enough working relationship with Bea, and that perhaps the program also lacked the support and relational means she felt were necessary for Bea to benefit from it.

Understanding this, it also did not escape our attention that it was due to her dismissal from that program and the advice of her teacher/counselor that Bea did seek out an intensive therapy that enabled her to engage in a more vital integrative process. This is ironic on two counts. On one point, it shows that Bea actually *did* trust her counselor and her advice, even though the counselor partly dismissed her for having a lack of trust. Secondly, the dismissal and advice for remedial therapy actually *did* work in Bea's favor as intended. There is a temptation to judge the program counselor as either *wrong* for not diagnosing

Bea in a more holistic, intersubjective manner or as *right* for referring her out for personal psychotherapy. However, from a contemplative perspective, both of these judgments miss the point. While the point of calculative diagnosing may indeed focus on distinguishing between what is right and wrong in the sense of "either/or," contemplative diagnosing seeks to open the mind and heart to the free play of awareness and the potentiality of "ands." Within an opened and opening field of inter-being, the play of discrimination intertwines with that of empathic resonance and is most oriented toward strengthening the capacity of self and other to more deeply embody an undistracted, unconditional presence.

Inter-being and the Challenge of Non-doing

Recognizing that Others do not exist independently of our consciousness of them, but only appear *within* an intersubjective field of consciousness, mindful awareness opens the door to a more saturated, undefined and undefinable, co-presencing. Rather than emphasizing conceptual understanding and elaboration of a particular fixation or self-world construct, meditative knowing emphasizes being present to the paradoxical Otherness of Self-fixations and Self-constructs. This process- and awe-based approach proceeds by letting beings be the beings they are, by offering the Other a relational field and vision that does not cling to any particular content, thus allowing for the natural release of fixations. In this, there is nothing special we need to do. In fact, *letting be presents us with the challenge of non-doing.*

Contemplative letting be does not neglect fixations by drifting into distraction or psychic numbness. Neither is it a discursive thinking about them. Rather, it involves taking the time to let the open awareness in which fixations and insights arise remain open. Whatever understandings arise within an inquiry need not be separated from the spacious field within which they emerge. Being unmediated, understanding does not lose touch with its impermanent nature. Thus, knowing is direct (*gnosis*). Since knowledge of an Other is not separated from its essentially open nature, it is not limited in any fundamental way. Thus, it is thorough (*dia*). So, a *diagnosis* that is true to the transience and interness of the subjective field in which it arises does not finally mean anything in particular, nor does it lack any particular meaning. Since this is the case, the knowing of other minds can be practiced as a kind of humble, loosening play.

Whether within the clinical practice of psychotherapy, non-clinical psycho-spiritual disciplines, or just in everyday life, how we approach knowing other minds reveals the limitations of our own mind. Seeing others according to the preconceptions of our own constructs obscures both the Otherness of the Other and the openness of our own self-world. If we only see what we have already conceived, then we will see only our preconceptions (projections). If our intention is to liberate ourselves (and others) from constraints, confusions, and conflicts of dualistic vision, we are challenged to shift from *knowing-about* (things, others, ourselves) to *knowing-with* the mysterious way things appear. This is the contemplative scientific challenge of bearing unconditional presence.

Of course, exercising unconditional awareness and putting the art of relational *non-doing* into practice takes considerable practice. Most of us do not fall out of bed one fine morning finding ourselves free of grasping and joyful friends with groundlessness! The strengthening of our capacity for bearing—and playing in—the lightness and darkness of *being* is required. By "strengthening," I mean both more thoroughly understanding the approach of mindful attunement and the increasing confidence that comes through putting it into practice. Because we live in a divided self-world habituated to materialism and proliferating conceptualizations, in order to practice in accord with a holistic vision, it is necessary to de-habituate from dualistic presuppositions and habituate to nondual awareness.

Phenomenological philosophy offers a potent holistic alternative to Cartesian dualism. However, philosophical study and calculative knowing in general is insufficient for *realizing* the vision phenomenology presents. Beyond intellectual understanding is the challenge of embodying nondual awareness. For this kind of attunement, it is necessary to practice non-conceptual, non-grasping openness and non-hesitating, non-striving responsivity. Contemplative spiritual traditions offer time-honored experiential *paths* for cultivating one's ability to be unconditionally present in the flux of time. However, the ancient Asian (often authoritarian-structured) spiritual traditions have not developed relationally interactive practices that are often invaluable for penetrating self-deception and promoting relational honesty. The development of a contemplative science challenges researchers, teachers, and clinicians alike to intertwine a personal practice of meditative awareness with the development of relational competencies. Not only this, but also to understand that the purpose of such an intertwining—like sheaves of wheat bound together with twine—is to be unbound, letting the sheaves fall where they may.

CHAPTER FOUR

On the Question of Sanity

*In order to understand estrangement, we must
understand that from which we are estranged,
namely our essential nature.*

—Paul Tillich

*We live in illusion and the appearance of things.
There is a reality. You are that reality. When you
understand this, you see that you are nothing, and
being nothing, you are everything. That is all.*

— Kalu Rinpoche

Given the focus on clinical diagnosis, the foregoing chapters inevitably accord to the discourse of clinical psychology and psychopathology. Even with a more informed understanding of the essential meaning of the word, why else "diagnose" someone if not to identify their particular illness, disorder, deficiency, stuckness, or problem(s)? In contrast, if the intention in understanding the mind of another person is to more deeply know him or her as they are in their wholeness and not merely in terms of their pathology, we typically do not refer to this kind of knowing in terms of diagnosis, but as an expression of "genuine interest," "love," or "appreciative discernment" (*prajna*).

A contemplative, "heart to heart" approach to the knowing of other minds requires that we enter the occasion as Rollo May advised, with "at least the readiness to love the other person, broadly speaking" (1958, p.38). When we relax the objectivizing, experience-distant mindset of empiricism and adopt instead an intersubjective, experience-near attitude, we are more able to access the subjectivity qua subjectivity of the other person. As the field of psychology now generally recognizes, empathic attunement is especially facilitative in encouraging another person to reveal more of him or herself to us (Prendergast, 2007), thus improving our knowing of them. The enhanced clarity and compassion that arises through being with an Other in a contemplative attitude influences the relational field in that direction. That is, the direction in which meditative discernment tends is toward what Chogyam Trungpa (2005) refers to as "*basic sanity*". This brings us to the question: What *is* basic sanity?

Conditional Sanity and Social Context

Psychology has ever-expanding inventories of psychopathology, such that the *DSM* is a metastasizing compendium proliferating mental disorders. It now is of a size that makes for an able doorstop. Deviating from the roman numeral versions of the preceeding *DSMs* (-*II*, -*III*, and -*IV*), the 2013 version is numbered *DSM-5*. This is a deliberate change which has been made to allow for the already anticipated continuing revisions of the *DSM as 5.1, 5.2, 5.3*, and so on. Although the *DSM-5* revision has taken well over a decade to complete, its authors knew prior to its publication that it was an incomplete and indefinite instrument unable to stand the test of even a short period of time.

Not only this, but theories of the causation of mental illness—from developmental to social to bio-chemical to trauma-based and beyond—are likewise expanding at an impressive rate. Not to be left behind, treatments of mental disorders are in a formidable growth curve, with pharmaceuticals, psychotherapies, somatic therapies, behavioral therapies, cognitive therapies, and various and sundry forms of self-help counseling doing a brisk business to meet an ever-growing demand of a modern world going, apparently, ever more crazy. Psychology has neglected the nature of sanity, including the mystery of human being and the phenomenology of spiritual awakening, for the noisier agitations of the distressed mind and the more readily available knowledge and power that comes from tossing ever more wood on the bonfire of insanities.

There is little comprehension of the nature of the mind and only nascent psychological inventories of sane qualities and potentialities (For example, Hutchins, 2002 & Sovatsky, 1998). While developments such as "positive psychology" are working to rectify this, such efforts focus on the qualities of positive mind states rather than on the nature of mind as such. Although mental disorders or illnesses are conceived as deviations from a presumed mental orderliness or healthiness, there is no consensually agreed-upon understanding as to what constitutes mental order or mental health. I will venture to address this lacuna by first identifying the ambiguous assumptions underlying the notion of mental health/order.

In particular, this chapter considers how the orderliness of everyday sanity is a social construct that maintains the status quo of consensual reality at the expense of the authentic, or essential, sanity of the person conforming to that reality. Sanity as conventionally understood is strictly relative to the social context which construes it. To understand a cultural construction of sanity is to understand something about the norms and mores of a particular culture, but not necessarily to understand anything at all about the nature or potentialities of unconstructed sanity.

There is the story of a good and wise king ruling over a faithful and prosperous kingdom that illustrates the core dilemma of relative sanity. From a fine, spring-fed castle on a hill, the king contentedly surveys the fields, dales, and villages of his realm. Then a strange event happens, as the rivers and wells of the lowlands become infected with a virus causing madness throughout the land. The king's subjects begin to hallucinate and speak in a strange way, making no apparent sense. Stranger still, they are somehow able to accord with each other in their shared madness. While they are not as productive as before, they still manage to continue their work and lives well enough. Of course, the king and his doctors do everything they can to cure the illness, but to no avail. Gradually, a gulf forms between the king and the people: he remaining perfectly sane while they babble on in their delusion, with neither side able to communicate with the other. The people come to see that their king is different from them and that he keeps himself aloof in his castle, speaking when he does in a strange and frightening tongue. In this estranged situation the people become increasingly suspicious of and alienated from their king, fomenting confusion and agitation. The king realizes he is at risk of losing his kingdom, so decides to drink the tainted water himself. In so doing, he also becomes quite mad, of course, but it is a madness shared by his subjects, who are soon relieved that their king is no longer acting so odd, and can once again rule benevolently over them.

There are many anthropological examples in which one culture's apparently sane, everyday norm is another culture's crazed abomination, decidedly abnormal and perhaps morally reprehensible. To observe but one instance, European explorers of the New World encountered what for the Aztecs and Incans was a perfectly normal and morally legitimate custom of making animal and human sacrifices to propitiate unseen gods. The Europeans found these rituals to be an ignorant, morally misguided, and spiritually bereft display of a kind of madness, something like a culture-wide irrational thought disorder. Christian missionaries replaced this madness with the Eucharist ritual of drinking the symbolic blood and eating the symbolic flesh of a brilliant young Jew executed 16 centuries earlier, which seemed to them to be a perfectly sane and reasonable transubstantiation of dead flesh into the living spirit of an unseen God. Of course, it is not hard to imagine that non-Christians, including some Jews themselves, find this practice to be an compulsive exercise in delusion, a bizarre religious ritual, and perhaps a kind of contagious, irrational thought disorder.

Even though sanity is relative to the culture which construes it, within its cultural context, the social construction defining sanity-madness reigns as absolute. (See Bennett, 1978; Foucault, 1965/1961; Laing, 1967; Szasz, 1974.) To deviate from a culture's definition of sanity is to court madness within that culture. The folk wisdom in the story of the mad king conveys that it is at times wise "to go along in order to get along," teaching that it can be useful to compromise one's own truth in order to maintain one's personal ties and social position in the service of social adaptation. The king wanted to continue being king and understood that in order to do so he could not continue to see things in his own seemingly sane way, but had to join in the madness of his realm. The price of being found relatively sane and so accepted by others was the loss of his sanity. That these Others are his own people well reflects the human condition. It is our own people in each our own family that form the (constructed) world into which we are born and to which we must adapt. As Freud observed (1961/1930), the price of social adaptation is psychological discontent, since the individual is compelled to contort, deny, or otherwise stifle his personal desires in order to belong to society. Whereas Freud focused exclusively on the self-restriction of sexual and aggressive impulses, self-restriction also extends to the suppression of more subtle impulses, such as the desire for authenticity and spiritual awakening when these desires emerge at odds with cultural norms. Heidegger refers to the voluntary—even if unconscious—suppression of authenticity as *losing oneself* in a world of otherness. As he laments, "Everyone is the other and no one is himself." (1962/1927, p.165)

Echoing Existential and cultural thinkers before and after him, Heidegger observes that a self who unwittingly conforms to a social context becomes lost in what he refers to as "the They" (*das Man*). The They is the anonymity of society: everybody and nobody, which cling to a particular worldview. In becoming submerged in this anonymity, authentic presence is lost. Every culture has its own view of the world, and different cultures, subcultures, and families are more or less rigid in the policing of that view. Depending on the rigidity of a worldview and the capacities of its members to tolerate differences, mysteries, and insecurities, groups have varying tolerance for what lies outside the constructs of their shared reality. Above all, it is the mission of the They to maintain the consensus vision which makes sense out of the dizzying immensity of existence, creating a coherent world in which a people can feel emotionally secure and mentally sane. As Ortega y Gasset puts it:

> For life is at the start a chaos in which one is lost. The individual suspects this, but he is frightened at finding himself face to face with this terrible reality, and tries to cover it over with a curtain of fantasy, where everything is clear. It does not worry him that his "ideas" are not true, he uses them as trenches for the defenses of his existence, as scarecrows to frighten away reality. (1985/1930, p.156.)

To quell existential anxieties, it is not necessary that social constructs be true, only that they be effective; and a worldview is only effective to the extent it is unquestioned.

History is littered with the steep price many self-honest men and women have paid for daring to express truths that emerge from a free mind, sourcing themselves from within rather than in conformity to the They. The terror that societies feel, and the terrorist acts the They deploy toward those they fear is written throughout the long arc of history. Unwilling to face each their own existential anxiety, individuals abrogate their freedom and responsibility, submerge themselves into the rabid anonymity of the pack, and so satisfy appetites of aggression that serve as sedation from a sobriety that might recognize the illusory nature of constructed reality. Socrates, Jesus, and witch hunts are but a few glaring examples of the intolerance the They has for nonconformity, especially if the nonconformity is not merely reactive, but a proactive force sourced from an individuating being.

In the modern world, largely by virtue of the rapid advances in technology and globalization, there are many forces acting to splay the cohesiveness of any particular worldview, raising tacit questions about the nature of reality and one's place within it. In what W. H. Auden has called "the age of anxiety," this creates a situation of increasing uncertainty and insecurity, giving rise both to the hope of a collective global village and fear of the loss of one's securely delimited sense of self and world. To decrease the anxieties stemming from a breakdown of a cohesive worldview, the They works to maintain the status quo by tranquilizing and deterring impulses of wakefulness that threaten the easy slumber of its consensual security arrangements. Various diversions promoting social cohesion at the expense of authenticity include many forms of mass entertainment, material acquisition, self-promotion, and the vapid,

self-absorbed "empty speech" of social chatter (twitter?).
All such preoccupations serve to distract us from who,
what, and where we actually are, and from where we are
going as we pass through time.

Existential Givens, Buddhist-style

Being lost in the They occurs in a sleep of what Heidegger
refers to as "average everydayness" (1962/1927, p.163-168),
which is an illusion we cultivate in order to avoid facing
unnerving truths of existence. The Buddha described three
existential characteristics with which every human being
must reckon: *suffering, impermanence,* and *no self.* While
it was common for Existential writers of the 20th Century
to posit various collections of existential givens with which
human beings must contend, all of these, such as anxiety,
meaninglessness, and death, are contained in these three
characteristics. Insofar as we keep ourselves benumbed,
stimulated, and generally preoccupied with relatively
meaningful activities, which means relatively meaningless
activities, then we are less likely to notice how we are, who
we are, and where we are bound. This everyday, seemingly
sane and apparently moral lack of awareness is what the
Buddha famously referred to as the primary *ignorance*
resulting in unnecessary suffering, and which Heidegger
referred to as the proximal cause of inauthenticity.

The primary characteristic of human existence

enshrined as the Buddha's first "noble truth" is the inescapable fact of *suffering*. That mortal suffering is inescapable does not, however, mean we do not try to do so. Suffering is obviously something we try to avoid when we get things we *do not* want, such as travel delays, indigestion, domestic discord, or illnesses great and small. We also do not want to suffer the infirmities and indignities of aging, and most especially we do not wish to die. Psychoanalysis understands this much. However, we also suffer when we get the things we *do* want, be it a beloved companion, a dear child, more money, a new technological gadget, a piece of jewelry, or even a sublime spiritual experience. These desirables turn out to be causes of suffering because once we have them we don't want to lose them. We suffer to the extent we seek to possess them and worry about their injury and loss. So we suffer both when we get what we don't want as well as when we get what we do want. If we take stock of this predicament, we come up against the paradoxical dilemma that unhappiness and dissatisfaction is caused both by our efforts to secure happiness and satisfaction and by trying to avoid the unhappiness and dissatisfaction inherent in existence. Surely this is crazy. Nevertheless, it is generally considered to be completely normal and perfectly sane to pursue and cling to our desires while avoiding and rejecting our aversions. And, in a consumption-driven society like ours, undeterred striving for material acquisition is even conceived of as a righteous endeavor.

Who can forget that following the shattering 9/11 air attacks on America, the President at the time, G. W. Bush, urged Americans to go shopping, lest the economy falter in a pause of material consumption. Rather then pause to more thoroughly digest the tragedy, understand its causes, and weigh an informed response, the country (the They) effectively closed down, submerging its vulnerability in arguably chaotic and reckless self-defensive aggressive reactions. In an effort to feel less vulnerable and more secure, the United States engaged in acts of war, torture, and political intrigue that alienated allies, energized enemies, and wound up only making Americans feel more afraid and less secure than before these impulsive self protective efforts began. Of course, one reason Americans experienced an extreme spike of insecurity following those brutal attacks was due to the American people's denial of being so vulnerable to terrorist attacks in the first place. America existed in a consensual illusion of invulnerability while actually existing in what had become a world increasingly vulnerable to such attacks. This is an example of how the They exists within "a curtain of fantasy" which seeks to avoid facing life's insecurities.

Even though it is a complete illusion to think that existential suffering can be avoided, the consensus opinion is that it is perfectly sane to try. Consider the eight everyday "worldly concerns," which the Buddha specified as sources of potential suffering whenever we believe that our well-being hinges on possessing one while avoiding the other: *pleasure and pain, praise and blame, gain and loss, and good versus bad reputation.* Striving to have pleasure and avoid pain is utterly sane and normal, is it not? Yet how can one be sensitive enough to delight in pleasure without also being sensitive to the agony of pain as well? When is it possible to be in love without running the risk of having that love be unrequited or falling out of love? Wanting to be praised but not blamed, seeking gain without loss, or wanting to be admired without being envied are all normal preferences which are impossible to have without also having its unwanted twin. All of these normal desires are like wishing to have "up" without "down." How sane is that? Upon even a little reflection we see that gain without loss is a fantasy, as is admiration without envy. These preferences are all futile exercises inviting more misery, yet they reflect the everyday sanity of the They.

Regarding the second existential characteristic, we exist wholly in a dimension of *impermanence.* We are just now—reading this sentence—hurtling through time on our way toward certain death. In addition to the favored distractions of a particular culture, and in our case we surely have many more possibilities for distraction than have ever before existed, there are the commonplace misdirections which Robert Stolorow refers to as "absolutisms of everyday life" (2007, p.13-16). By this, he refers to the common incantations we recite to reinforce an illusion of security covering over our inherently insecure existence. These absolutisms include such everyday affirmations as "I'll see you later" to a friend, or "I'll see you tomorrow" when tucking in a child for the night, or "I'll be right back" to our partner as we leave on a short errand. Of course, we have no idea whether or not these assurances are true. We do know that some day, although we know not which day, they most certainly will not be true. But we ignore the fact that we know we do not know what awaits us as leave the house each morning. In fact, we do not even know what will happen if we stay home for the day and merely climb in and out of the shower, light the stove, descend the stairs, and answer the doorbell on a perfectly ordinary day...a day like any other day. Marvelously, assuming that nothing unexpected will occur and life will proceed without inter-ruption, we readily deny the truth of impermanence by warmly offering and eagerly accepting these reassurances to and from each other. In so doing we collude in servicing an illusion of permanence.

In regard to the third characteristic, still more strongly do we cling to the view of consensus reality that supports the illusion that our selfhood is a solid ground in an oth-erwise chaotic sea of change and Otherness. In addition to the existential truths of suffering and impermanence, the Buddha observed there is the ontological truth of *self-lessness*. At first glance, this declaration seems strange and simply wrong. That "I" exist as an enduring entity seems to be the most incontrovertible fact of existence, the denial of which at first strikes us as either absurd or nihilistic. Indeed, Buddhism has been faulted, mistakenly, as a nihilistic religion. As with all the Buddha's teachings, this declaration too is not to be taken passively as an article of faith. The point is not to *believe* it, but to *discover* if it is true. Meditative inquiry into the nature of the self is a powerful lens through which to discern the nature of unconstructed sanity as distinct from social constructions of sanity that vary from context to context.

Having tired of years of ascetic exercises trying to improve himself, Siddhartha Gautama sat on a comfortable seat under a sheltering tree and engaged in simple and straight-forward self-inquiry. During his long night of self-reckoning, he discovered the brilliant nature of sanity itself. In recognizing and releasing the distorting tendencies of his mental fixations and emotional conflicts, he discovered that the cessation (*nirvana*) of clinging to the self constructs of relative sanity was in itself a bliss-saturated freedom surpassing all conceptual understanding. Letting go of the fear, aggression, and grasping of his emotionally-fueled firm convictions, the constructed existence of his selfhood separate from the Otherness of the world collapsed into unimpeded openness and spontaneous responsivity, which is referred to as an *awakening* to the way things actually are. The way things actually are in the interdependent connectedness of existence is decidedly not how we construe them according to our self-centered imaginings. A non-self-centered awakening refers to a kind of individuation virtually unimaginable to conventional Psychology.

Whether examining the minds of ourselves or others, we readily find that it is a separate sense of Self which forms the primary identity and personal territory which we defend against the intrusions and unpredictable Otherness of the world. The insulation of a separate self and delimited world is a marvelous fiction, creating a habitable self-world that is—within its constructs—comprehensible and predictable. In child development, we know very well that if a child is unable to create a dependable sense of self, that child will feel extraordinary powerlessness and be increasingly vulnerable to psychic fragmentation. Given the transient immensity of existence, it is no wonder that we are developmentally prone to "cover [chaos] over with a curtain of fantasy, where everything is clear." And then, to cling to our constructions "as scarecrows to frighten away reality." Especially as children, the vastness of existence can certainly feel overwhelming, and it is of utmost importance for caretakers to sooth the existential anxieties of children with the reassurance, illusory though it may be, that "everything is going to be fine." But also as adults, people have varying capacities for tolerating unknowing, Otherness, and the disturbing givens of existence. It is important to respect that the constructs of consensual sanity serve a protective function, and not everybody at anytime has the capacity to accept the mysterious, potentially terrifying and potentially wondrous truths about themselves and temporal existence.

As Carl Jung is to have said, "The most terrifying thing is to accept oneself completely." When we look deeply into the nature of the self we take ourselves to be, it can be disturbing to accept what we find in two senses. Psychologically, we are challenged to accept the egoic humiliation that we are not entirely how we like to think of ourselves but bear an unconscious "shadow" of disowned intentions, impulses, and ideas that may be chaotic, humiliating, threatening, or otherwise disruptive of our conscious, cohesive senses of self. Ontologically, the matter is more serious, since in seeing that "I" am no thing— not the firm ground of being I take myself to be—I am up against the vertigo of groundlessness. Heidegger, echoing the Buddha, spoke to this situation suggesting that not only do we who are lost in the They wish to ignore the truth that we will die one day, we are even more keen to ignore the truth that we are not self-existing just now! Distraction in idle activities and relatively meaningless pursuits serve as a hedge against discovering the groundlessness, or as the Existentialists provocatively put it, the *abyss* of self and world. Even though Heidegger glimpsed and the Buddha realized that the discovery of selflessness opens a way to the freedom and bliss of inter-being, accepting such openness can be a formidable challenge.

Existential Anxiety

Both Freud and Heidegger spoke to the difference between fear and anxiety. They each specify that fear is always *fear of* something, an "entity-within-the-world" as Heidegger put it. The something might be an actual thing that is about to happen or it might be something that is imagined. In either case there is an entity or event that is feared. In the face of fear, it is possible to mount defenses to combat the identifiable threat (whether or not it actually exists). One's response to fear may be skillful or misguided, but either way one is mobilized to either action or inaction—fight or flight or freeze—that rivets attention to the what that is feared, binding attention to an external object.

Anxiety, on the other hand, is not about an objective entity or event, but is about one's own subjective being, which is no thing. Anxiety is "completely indefinite…nothing and nowhere," and yet this non-being is "being-in-the-world as such" (Heidegger, as quoted in Stolorow, 2011, p.36). There is a marked difference between observable or knowable things and the *being* of the being who observes and knows these things. As Heidegger put it, a human being is "distinguished by the fact that, in its very Being, that Being is an *issue* for it" (1962/1927, p.32). That is, one's very existence is a mystery, an unresolved issue which niggles, drawing one's attention within. As one senses into the no-thingness which is oneself, one may feel a kind of dizziness. Whether by deliberately inquiring into the enigma of oneself or in being haunted by an existential disquiet, perhaps arising unbidden in the middle of the night, one finds oneself *anxious*. As Kierkegaard observed, "anxiety is the dizziness of freedom." Heidegger felt that confronting existential anxiety is an individuating opportunity in which one is compelled to turn from the superficialities of everydayness to the actualities of existence. Buddhism speaks of this turning toward the way things actually are as "noble," while Existentialists refer to it as "authentic."

Paradoxically, the process of individuation evokes existential anxiety precisely because of its release of self-groundedness. We typically think of individuation as the development of a separate selfhood. Whereas, to the extent it is an existentially authentic process, individuation involves the de-centering of self-centeredness along with a growing capacity to tolerate unsettledness and non-self-centeredness. Authentic subjectivity discovers it is an occasion of *inter*subjectivity. As one becomes more oneself, relaxing more deeply into the who, what, and where one actually is, the inherent open/inter-ness of selfhood becomes more apparent.

The Impulse of Authenticity

Although we tend to lose ourselves in the They, we can never completely escape the sanity of our basic nature.

The unconditioned openness of inter-being exerts a gravitational pull which I call *the impulse of authenticity*. Unnervingly, this impulse is at once a pull toward toward unconstructed sanity and relative insanity (defined according to the They).

There seems to be no way around the paradox that there is madness in sanity as well as sanity in madness. Since the relative sanity of social reality serves as a brace against the enduring actualities of existential reality, everyday reality is in some sense mad. At the same time, madness is often the breakthrough of a sane intelligence that screams or withdraws or otherwise insinuates to oneself and others that living inauthentically as a They-self is untenable. For instance, the dissociating mind that refuses to psychically submit to abuse or rape and so be treated as a mere object of plunder, ridicule, or worse, has an intelligent integrity to it. Or, the ADHD (Attention Deficit Hyperactivity Disorder) that refuses to sit still, keep quiet, and behave itself, but thrashes out from a chaos of over-stimulated disembodied disquiet, emotional malattunement, and anxious estrangement from the natural world, vividly expresses the intoxicating speed and aggression that can come from living disattached in an experience-distant virtual reality. Or again, consider the schizophrenia which is unable and/or unwilling to either accept or ignore the hidden hypocrises, double-bind confusion, and willful ignorance of the world. The schizophrenic is considered to be crazy in being overly sensitive to everyday deceptions, pretense, and confusing hypocrisies, and thereby escaping the brutal dissimulation of shared reality for a separate reality where things make sense, even if it is a terrifying sense.

What is considered to be a "Disorder" is actually quite orderly and well-organized, often making definite sense within one's particular self-world construct. When observed closely, it can be seen that the organization of madness is an intelligent attempt to manage and make some kind of sense out of otherwise unreognized, consensual forms of madness. In so doing, madness may, however awkwardly, painfully, and irritatingly, express a potentiality for authentic presence.

The impulse of authenticity is something we can either accept, ignore, or deny. To the extent we ignore or reject it, authenticity tugs at our conscience, nags at us as anxiety, guilt, or despair. So that even when things are going momentarily well, we still feel vaguely incomplete and somehow wanting, craving for our situation to either not change or to be further improved. On the other hand, to the extent that we accept this impulse, or "summons," as Heidegger poignantly puts it, and bear the anxiety that arises in so doing, the sanity of unconditional presence is more enabled to arise in our mindstreams.

In the search for and acceptance of authenticity, it is helpful to recognize at the outset that essential sanity cannot be found in conceptual constructs, be they philosophical, psychological, or religious. Just as the seeds of madness arise from everyday sanity, seeds of genuine sanity arise from madness. While this situation is completely ironic, if we are honest with ourselves, everything hinges on our willingness to suffer the actuality of this vertigo as we release clutching onto the familiar ground of our firm ideas and opinions. This means we are challenged to open up the way we think things are—in terms of the everyday constructs which divvy existence into dualistic notions of either/or, thises vs. thats—and confront the way things actually are. That is, we must allow ourselves to be open and unconstructingly present, at least for a time.

When Heidegger refers to our own *being* as the core *issue* of human being, he identifies to my way of thinking, the overarching purpose of being human. To the extent this concern remains unaddressed, we have not fully realized the purpose of life and so continue to feel somehow incomplete and to suffer some measure of existential anxiety. As the Buddha discovered, to come to complete terms with this issue leads to its dissolution and the evaporation of anxieties.

Existential thought is not so bold as to go this far. Like psychoanalysis, it is wary of self-deception and suspicious of claims to the effect, as well as the possibility of, "fully realizing" life's purpose. And for good reason. It is very appealing to the They-self to fool itself into thinking it is beyond existential insecurities in having attained the ultimate ground of being, resulting in all manner of religious and political zealotry, ego-inflation, spiritual bypassing, and a recalcitrant form of existential lostness in which one becomes convinced one is not lost. Of course, meditation masters are also well aware of this pitfall. Nevertheless, being aware of the pitfall does not mean that the impulse of authenticity is exhausted when one is courageous enough to face up to existential truths.

Having dared existential sobriety, there is still the matter of living authentic presence forward, both in relationship to others and in regard to reckoning with one's own unrealized potentialities of authentic presentness. Seeing suffering, impermanence, and selflessness as the way things actually are does not mean one has completely resolved one's issues with this situation and is able to fully integrate this knowledge. Beyond glimpsing the empty-openness of our basic nature lies the challenge of embodying this unconditioned presence in everyday life. From what I can tell, such reckoning and integration are the *key issues* (*raison d'etre*) of human being. All other reasons and activities are secondary or preparatory to the primary purpose of recognizing, embodying, and radiating brilliant sanity.

Again, there is a difference between the psychological integration of unconscious material and an ontological recognition of one's true nature. Summarizing the psychoanalytic project of "making the unconscious conscious," Jung wrote that psychological integration involved a "transcendent function" which is a "bringing together of opposites for the production of a third [position, in which]…it is no longer the unconscious that takes the lead but the ego" (1969/1957, p.67-91). This "third" position involves a synthesis of conscious and unconscious attitudes into a less divided selfhood. However, this psychological integration, as valuable as it is for coming to better terms with one's inner divisions and so providing a more stable position from which to inquire more deeply into the nature of one's being, is not yet recognition of that essential nature.

The discovery of basic sanity (*rig-pa*), which the Dzogchen master Chogyal Namkhai Norbu translates as "primordial awareness" or "instantaneous, nondual presence" (Namkhai Norbu & Clemente, 1999, p.58), is not a unification of opposites, but the intrinsically undivided nature which allows for both the division and unification of opposites. From this perspective, the positing of a transcendent function is superfluous, since there is nothing to transcend. *The search for and realization of authenticity is not the attainment of a particular **state**, but a **process** of increasing attunement.* Through attuning to the impulse of authenticity, one de-integrates from (protective) self and world constructs to which one unconsciously clings, which is simultaneously an opening to the essential inter-ness of being in time. In being-open, one is more able to integrate whatever arises within the presence of basic wakefulness. This integrative process is easily misunderstood, inviting further clarification.

Unconditioned Sanity:
Its Essence, Nature, and Energy

Explicated according to the Dzogchen tradition of Vajrayana Buddhism, basic sanity, or instant presence, has three aspects: *essence, nature, and energy* (Namkhai Norbu, 1986, p.56-73). While these are experientially indistinguishable, they can be conceptually teased out in order to better understand the subtle and elusive nature of unconditioned mind.

As has been discussed, the *essence* of mind is empty-openness (*sunyata*). Without center or periphery, the mind is essentially an unconstructed capacity of inter-ness, vast like an unclouded sky. Far from being a mere "void," as *sunyata* has sometimes been translated, the *nature* of empty-openness is cognizant liveliness.[4] Like every other sense organ, it is the nature of the mind (understood as the sixth sense organ in Buddhist psychology) to perceive. Unlike other sense organs, the mind's perceptions include conceptions, and concepts have the unique power of appropriating perceptions of the other five senses by interpreting them according to various criteria and intentions. The cognizant quality of mind therefore has the capacity to either disregard its essential openness, which includes the sensory experiences appearing within it, or not. In disregard (or ignorance) of its true nature, the mind detaches from being-in-the-world and seems (to itself) to exist separate from the world. It is not recognized that this split occurs wholly as the mind's own construction. This ignoring, and self-managing of experience, is a form of intentionality which the Buddha identified as the root cause of suffering (ie. *samsara*).

By grasping onto what is liked, rejecting what is disliked, and ignoring what is of no personal interest, one participates in an on-going struggle with one's self-world. Since self and world are not fundamentally separate, the tensions of this struggle are felt to be inner tensions, manifesting as self-conflicts. The solidified split between self and world, including self and other, can be understood as *basic insanity*, which may then develop into more sophisticated manifestations of psycho-somatic pathology. At the same time, since the nature of mind is essentially open and free like the sky, even though clouds (of conceptual formulations) may obscure its empty essence, the mind's cognizant quality can always rediscover and recognize its intrinsic non-self-centered spaciousness (Wegela, 1994).

When mind recognizes that the nature of sensory perceptions and mental constructs are in essence unconstructed, the apparent separation between self and world collapses, releasing mind's intrinsically healing energetic properties. The *energy* of mind manifests as nondualistic responsivity. In letting oneself be...and continue to be... open and undefended, with naked awareness not losing itself in the clothing of its perceptions, the impulse of authenticity expresses itself in discerning and compassionate responses to self and other. In contrast to everyday emotional reactivity that aims to defend or enhance a self-position, the energy of unconditional presence responds to experience without, or with reduced, self-centered distortion. Responding without attachment or aversion to what arises or passes away within the field of awareness loosens the tensions that bind one to a defensive position and the anonymity of the They.

Whether alone or with others, when the energy of nondual attunement is unimpeded, subtle psychic holdings that constrict body and mind in defensive-offensive postures naturally release. This occurs simply because the intentional effort that maintains them loosens. In Dzogchen, the naturally healing responsiveness of authentic presence is referred to as self-liberation (*rang-drol*) (Reynolds, 2000). In contrast to what is normally thought of as psychological or spiritual "work" involving earnest effort, the natural resilience of basic sanity delivers its healing power through the "play" of effortless presencing. The maintenance of self-defensiveness, self-image, and conformity to the security arrangements of the They requires an on-going exercise of intention. Releasing the tensions of defensive intentionality involves not practicing them for at least a moment or two. It is in a pause of self-intending that fundamental healing takes place, as the subtle effort maintaining dualistic vision relaxes. Ironically, it is by relaxing one's efforts to secure oneself that one is able to discover that there is nothing to be secure from. One need not worry about what cannot be secured in the first place. Naturally resilient sanity cannot be created, neither can it be destroyed. It can however be released from fixating tendencies which obscure and bind it.

This brief discussion of unconditioned sanity sketches a conceptual understanding of the essence, nature, and energy of mind, and is not at all the same as arriving at an alive experiential understanding, which is a trans-rational wisdom. To access such living wisdom it is indispensable to find a qualified teacher of nondual presence who has experiential understanding him or herself.

Conclusion

The deceptively simple message of psychological practices informed by basic sanity is "let it be" (which Heidegger (1966/1959) refers to as *gelassenheit*). The irony of this is that the non-doing of letting be may be the most difficult thing we can ever do! It can seem impossible or feel terrifying to let go of our everyday sanitized consensual security arrangements, self-image management scenarios, and taken-for-granted worldviews. To let go of these is, in some measure, to risk our relative sanity, since it involves loosening to the point of unraveling the threads of our intentionality which weave the fictive fabric of our solid sense of self and world. Of course there are many skillful means that can be employed to guide, buffer, support, confront, soothe, and otherwise assist an opening to authentic presence, but that requires a much larger discussion. I am content here to sketch the paradox of sanity/insanity that a search for authenticity invokes. This leaves many avenues of inquiry open for further research, such as: Is it true that unconditioned presence has inherent healing potential?

Figure 1: Buddha displaying the earth-touching mudra

As a pointer for this kind of inquiry, there is an enduring image (Figure 1) that has served as an encouragement for many on the path of awakening: the classic figure of the seated Buddha having passed through the night of his enlightenment. He sits in dignified repose, the fingers of his right hand touching the ground. The "dark night of the soul" through which he has just passed opened him to the depths of suffering, the full fury of his hopes, fears, and confusions. Having emerged into the wakefulness of brilliant sanity in which confusion self-liberates, dawning as wisdom, he expressed this recognition simply by touching the ground upon which he sat. The usual explanation of this "earth-touching mudra" is that he was having the earth bear witness to his awakening. I find this explanation to be weak.

Resting in the boundless wakefulness and healing bliss[5] of unconditional presence, would the Buddha need a witness? I doubt that he needed any validation beyond the self-evidence of the intrinsic openness in which he then unwaveringly dwelt. My sense is the Buddha is expressing in this gesture the trans-conceptual actuality of awakening in the sense of displaying that everything is as it is. Nothing need be corrected, nothing need be enhanced. Touching the ground says simply and directly, just here in this place, just now at this time, everything is complete as it is. The upturned hand resting easy on his lap expresses the natural confidence of unobstructed openness: anything can be held lightly, any situation is manageable, just as it arises and passes away.

CHAPTER FIVE

Natural Resilience: A Heart Sutra for Psychotherapy

As the circle of science grows larger, it touches paradox at more places.

—Friedrich Nietzsche

Emptiness is not other than form, form is not other than emptiness.

—the Heart Sutra

What is usually referred to as *mindfulness-based* psychology draws upon the basic Buddhist meditation practice combining calm abiding (*shamatha*) with insight *(vipashyana)* into the true nature of mind and mental-emotional events. While mindfulness practice is foundational to all schools of Buddhism, it is exclusively emphasized in what is called Hinayana Buddhism. Within the Buddhist world, there are three grand approaches, or paths *(yanas)*: Hinayana, Mahayana, and Vajrayana. While the goal of each approach is the release of self-perpetuated suffering, the approaches to that release vary.

The Hinayana, or "lesser path," is better understood as the "fundamental path" to self-liberation. This approach emphasizes the practice of mindful concentration, insight, and self-responsibility born out of self-restraint. Its over-riding purpose is to cease creating misery for oneself and others. As the basic Buddhist path, it proceeds from the *samsara* of repetitive, heedless, and needless suffering to a *nirvana* in which such suffering comes to a decisive end.

Even as a foundational approach, the simple practice of self-attention exerts a formidable power for cutting through the self-ignorance and self-deception that unwittingly fuels many kinds of misery. Through the sustained cultivation of mindful awareness, a funny thing can happen on the way to *nirvana*. It turns out that through practicing mindfulness for oneself, one's heart may wider open as one finds oneself, perhaps unexpectedly, having increased concern with the welfare of others. Through meditative attunement, it is common for empathy to deepen, which of course is especially advantageous for experience-near, relationally-robust practices of psychotherapy. In the field of mindfulness psychology, this deepening is currently being reflected by an increasing emphasis on the valuing and cultivation of compassion in addition to insight alone. This heart-y development is indicative of the maturation of a Hinayana sensibility into a Mahayana sensitivity, which differs from the fundamental path in two key ways.

Mahayana translates as "greater path." However, "greatness" here does not mean that it is superior to the Hinayana. Rather, *maha*yana reflects a greater inclusivity in its vision as well as a broader range of applicable meditative practices. While the ideal of the Hinayana practitioner is the *Arhat* who, through his own efforts, ends once and for all his own suffering, the ideal of the Mahayana practitioner is the *Bodhisattva*, who puts the welfare and liberation of others on an even footing with, or even ahead of, his own release. Whereas mindful awareness is a key emphasis of basic Buddhism, compassion is a special emphasis of the Bodhisattva path. (The Dalai Lama is a prime example of the kindness displayed by a Bodhisattva.)

A more confounding difference of the Mahayana approach is the counter-intuitive recognition that *nirvana* is found nowhere else than in *samsara* itself. It seems that the mindfully opened and opening heart eventually recognizes that the reasonable and perfectly sane desire to escape suffering is itself a kind of avoidance and tacit aggression against both oneself as a flawed human being and this world as a vale of tears. On a path of robust compassion, we are challenged to not only attune to other persons, but to attune more kindly to the Otherness within ourselves. In order to more deeply release the conviction that we, being flawed, need to change or be released from who or how we are, we are challenged to not fight ourselves, but to more fully accept the flawed Otherness of ourselves as is.

In order to more fully and radically accept the being I am, I must be in greater accord with that being. In the heartfelt deepening of mindful attunement, the stark divisions between Self and Other, flawed self and ideal self, and *nirvana* and *samsara* become increasingly permeable to the point of illusory. If I do not succumb to self-deceptions such as spiritual bypassing, an increasingly saturated mindfulness spontaneously opens a door to an effortless release of striving for all kinds of self-improvement or self-liberation.

Although effortless liberation may be difficult to comprehend and presents us with a bold paradox, it nevertheless presents a path for awakening essential sanity of which Psychology would do well to better understand. One of the most succinct expositions of the wonder of effortless liberation is the Mahayana *Heart Sutra*. A pith teaching of logical paradox, it is sometimes referred to as the heart attack sutra for its ability to shatter all manner of tacit assumptions and mental constructs, leaving the reader awestruck, heart missing a beat open to the breathtaking groundlessness of time and being. While endeavoring to remain true to the meaning and meter of the classic Sutra, I have adapted this radical teaching to accord more closely to the vocabulary of psychology and practice of depth therapy.

If the Mahayana is broad, the vision and practices of the Vajrayana are broader still. Vajrayana literature is written in Tantras, as distinct from the Sutras of the Hina and

Mahayana, and its practices are considered to be more direct, and so more dangerous, in the sense that the release of the constructs of relative sanity are more abrupt and decentering. For our present purposes, grappling with that heart attack sutra, which already conveys the essence of the Vajrayana, is sufficient.

While deeply settled in a moment of perfect presence, a moment unlike any other moment, a moment as likely as any other moment, the Bodhisattva of Great Compassion, Avalokitesvara, looked into the motivation, the work and the goal of psychotherapy and found them equally empty and completely resilient. After this penetration, he overcame all confusion, doubt and hesitation.

"Listen," he said, "the motivation for being in therapy: having problems, stuckness or patholog-ical tendencies such as obsession, depression, and anxiety, does not differ from resilience, and the capacity for resilience does not exist apart from problems / stucknesses / pathological tendencies. As for therapeutic work, in doing therapy there is nothing particular to do. The resilient openness and responsiveness of shared presence is itself the doing of therapy. The work of therapy is nothing other than unconditional presence: the open and responsive play of being-with an other. The noble goal of depth psychotherapy, such as transforming what is unconscious into consciousness that is open and responsive in the world, is not other than naturally arising, unconditioned, primordially empty, resilience itself. There is neither someplace to reach nor a particular state to attain."

"Listen well, attendants of psyche, since problems do not exist apart from natural resilience, there is nothing to resolve and no way to resolve it. Since there is nowhere else to go and nothing particular to attain, there are no resistances, obstacles, or inadequacies to work through. Like an ice cube melting in warm water, resistance and problems dissolve in the self-arising resilience of mind and heart. Whoever understands this effortlessly releases the tensions of should or should not, ought to or ought not, and resting in natural resilience, slips beyond the waves of suffering, struggle, and doubt."

Commentary

The pithy adage, *you are what you eat*, makes much sense. Whether we eat organically grown or mass produced foods, we know we absorb the vitamins, minerals, nutrients, and chemicals contained in those foods, for good or ill. They enter our digestive system, our bloodstream, and pass into our muscles, skin, bones, and organs. Quite literally, we become that which we ingest. In a similar way, the Buddha taught that we are what we *think*. Just as physical food becomes inseparable from our physical body, the thoughts and beliefs we absorb, both as children and adults, become inseparable from our mental-emotional disposition. What we take in about ourselves and the world form and inform who we take ourselves to be and how we see others and the world. While food has obvious physical effects, the effects of held beliefs are more subtle. To discover the effects they have on our psychic well-being requires a more subtle kind of inquiry than we typically practice. Analytic and cognitive therapies can reveal gross cognitive distortions. Meditative practices, solo or interpersonal, enable inquiry into the more subtle psychological constructs that inform and limit our sense of self and world.

It is worth repeating that among the most essential discoveries of the Buddha, and perhaps the most difficult for us to comprehend, is the observation that the solid and enduring self I take to be me is a case of mistaken identity.

"I" am not as solid or enduring as my beliefs and memory suggest. The "I" that I take myself to be is nothing other than a web of emotionally charged mental constructs, which I have absorbed and become identified with. When I look deeply into the self which I consider "me," I find a subjective sense which may feel anxious, depressed, confused, relieved, or satisfied, but which does not exist as a discrete, autonomous entity. This subjective sense of self has no objective, independent existence in either time or space.

Nothing of this radical insight is contradicted by modern depth psychology. In speaking of "unconscious organizing principles" or "old patterns," and even in the subfield of *Self* psychology, there is no separate, discrete self to be found. What are spoken of are "matrices" of psychological "organization" or "patterns" of behavior, which may be traced back to formative relational experiences that were taken in and bound together to become a *structure* of subjectivity (Atwood & Stolorow, 1984). It is not the subjectivity that is enduring, but the *structuring* of subjective experience. Understanding that the self lacks any enduring existence, the Bodhisattva relaxes into a moment of simple stillness.

While deeply settled in a moment of perfect presence, a moment unlike any other moment, a moment as likely as any other moment, the Bodhisattva of Great Compassion looked into the motivation, the work and the goal of psychotherapy and found them equally empty and completely resilient.

A moment of perfect presence is a moment in which awareness floats freely and openly and is not identified with or reactive against any mental-emotional construct. Such a moment can happen at any time and, when it does, it has never happened before, which is why it can never be repeated, although it may be discovered repeatedly.

Clients often come to therapy feeling they have "lost it" in some way or are about to "lose it." Typically, we accept this at face value, recognizing and believing in their dread of losing themselves somehow. But the Bodhisattva is not so easily taken in. What is it after all, that might have been or might yet be lost? It cannot be the person's presence, their *being* that is lost or in danger of being lost, since presence, not being a physical or mental construction, can neither be created nor destroyed. So whatever the matter is, it is empty of any essential substance. A person might indeed feel panicked or dispirited about losing or lacking something felt to be essential, but the Bodhisattva is not tempted to become panicked or dispirited herself about this, since she realizes that "losing it" is the necessary precondition for finding it, whatever "it" is. Remaining unperturbed in a moment of perfect presence, she understands that since being found comes from being lost, and that liberation comes from being bound or stuck, the motive, work, and goal of therapy are all intrinsically resilient.

Resilience comes from *resilire*, which means "returning to the original position; springing back." It carries the flavor of a light touch, of flexibility or "springiness." However, it also often happens that under pressure we might spring back to an old, habitual position. But in this sense we would speak of reversion, or regression, rather than resilience. Reverting is a defensive contraction, a form of resistance which often feels rigid, fearful, or tight. It might even appear light, but in the sense of a "flight to light," a "spacey" disavowal or withdrawal in the face of a challenging encounter. On the other hand, the springiness of resilience is not a return to an earlier defensive position, but an expression of suppleness, of the capacity to relate creatively with whatever is difficult or alluring.

Essentially, resilience is a "return to the original position." So, in terms of psychology, what is the "original position" of the psyche? Following from the understandings of the Buddha, we could observe that since the structure of subjectivity is arbitrary, formed according to the constructs we have grown up ingesting, it is not original, but a secondary accretion. Originary human nature is unconstructed, as in *not yet* bound by any particular structure, but unstructured in the sense of unfixed, undefended, open, naked, pliable. So while the essence of human being is *open*: empty, receptive, unconditioned, the nature of this openness is *responsive*: relational, creative, resilient. Resilience being the natural capacity for springing back, leaning in, returning to a more open, undefended and responsive way of being with others and the world.

> "Listen", he said, "the motivation for being in therapy: having problems, stuckness, or pathological tendencies such as obsession, depression, and anxiety, does not differ from resilience, and the capacity for resilience does not exist apart from problems/stucknesses/pathological tendencies.

Being present with what is, the Bodhisattva sees that the core confusion which results in stucknesses or symptoms comes from the conviction that things ought to be other than they are. The sense that something about my life is "wrong" or lacking, or that I, or you, need to change, stems from resisting life as it actually is. Whatever my particular symptoms or suffering might be, the motivation for coming to therapy is to alleviate that suffering, which might include the desire to sublimate or transform it into some wisdom or emotional maturity. Whether I bluntly just want to get rid of a nagging depression for example, or more subtlety, want to explore my despair to divine its tacit psychological or spiritual meaning, and through this become a more individuated or enlightened person, the common denominator is that I want to change the way things are, the way I am living. The desire to change my life, or the way I am, is, of course, much more intelligent than doing nothing at all, proceeding through life like an ostrich living in denial or as a hapless slave of the conditioning beliefs and influences of the They. Still, the motivation for therapy is a desire to be in some way different, perhaps more resilient than I have been. The uncomfortable sense of stuckness, pain, or inadequacy which calls out to be released or fixed is itself the harbinger of resilience. How can this be?

Resilience arises where it is lacking. It is precisely those places where we are stuck, terrified, or resigned in despair that call forth resilience. Resolution can occur only where there is an unresolved conflict, otherwise there is nothing to resolve. The stuckness that begs to be loosened is that which invites loosening. In order to spring back and return to an original position, it is necessary to have lost touch with that position. It is only when we have gotten off-track or "lost our head" that we can exercise the resilience of turning and returning, of finding and re-cognizing. Only when we are out of touch is it possible to spring back in touch. Resilience cannot be found outside of problems, just as problems allow for and invite resilience. This suggests that I don't lack what I think I lack, am not as stuck as I feel I am, and need not struggle as much as I think I do.

> As for therapeutic work, in doing therapy there is nothing particular to do. The resilient openness and responsiveness of unconditional shared presence is itself the doing of therapy.

Neither validating or invalidating problems, pathologies, or struggles, the Bodhisattva of genuine compassion does not buy into the sense of psychological poverty that suggests there is something wrong or flawed about "me" or "my life." At the same time, he does not deny that there are compelling problems that do feel stuck and painful in some way. Without engaging a story of woe and without disengaging from it, we are more able to be with the problem as it is rather than how we think it is. This might be taken as a mandate to do nothing, but if that is what we are intentionally doing, then "nothing" becomes a something: we will have adopted a passive and perhaps avoidant position of inaction. This would be another kind of mental-emotional construction that obscures the original position of spacious openness and relational responsiveness. To be ready to respond or moved to respond, without feeling that we ought or ought not respond, is a moment of resilient

relationality. It is resilient in the sense that it is a kind of
play, like a well-oiled hinge has play. Therapeutic responses
are then not done by rote or with the effortful sense of
"work" which is aimed at accomplishing some task. Since
resilience cannot be created, there is no task that need be
done, and equally, no task that need not be done. Like the
serious work of children at play, the Bodhisattva advises
a similar attitude in the practice of psychotherapy, which
involves the supple play of listening and speaking from
what is.

> The noble goal of depth psychotherapy, such as
> transforming what is unconscious into conscious-
> ness that is open and responsive in the world, is not
> other than naturally arising, unconditioned, pri-
> mordially empty resilience itself. There is neither
> someplace to reach nor a particular state to attain.

If the goal of therapy is to be more conscious or more
functional or more open and responsive in the world,
where is this consciousness and functionality to be found?
And how do we get there? How could it ever be found any-
where but here and now? If I think my client is in a dis-
turbed or dysfunctional state, and even if she herself wants
to change a distraught state to a calmer one, where would

that better state be? If I think my client needs to get "there," to a better, less pathological place, I am putting her and myself with her in conflict with what actually exists. In doing this, I risk reinforcing her negative sense of herself as being flawed and collude with her in resisting the present moment, which is unfortunate, since it is the only moment either of us has. This aversion on the part of the therapist and the therapeutic ambition to "make things better," has been recognized as a display of "therapeutic aggression" which "is trying to get someone to change so that *we*, as helpers, can feel better" (Wegela, 2011, p.84).

The Bodhisattva realizes that by either validating or invalidating a particular problem or conflict, the therapist tends to reify, and perhaps strengthen that conflict. Trying to change a bad attitude for a better one maintains the inner conflict of striving for an idealized self while resisting a despised self. Even though there might be some therapeutic progress made in this way, it is unlikely that resilience will be evoked. Instead of evoking resilience, therapy then becomes a work of behavioral management and/ or attitude adjustment in which one is preoccupied with monitoring oneself or one's client to promote the good and renounce the bad. This is a recipe for perpetuating the struggle of striving for an ideal "I" who is other than who one actually is. While such work may be a viable step in a course of therapy, it nevertheless remains an activity of mental construction which does not yet elicit the play of natural resilience which enables a deeper, more thorough liberation from self and world constructs: the noble, radical heart of psychotherapy.

> "Listen well, attendants of psyche, since problems do not exist apart from natural resilience, there is nothing to resolve and no way to resolve it. Since there is nowhere else to go and nothing particular to attain, there are no resistances, obstacles or inadequacies to work through. Like an ice cube melting in warm water, resistance and problems dissolve in the self-arising resilience of mind and heart. Whoever understands this effortlessly releases the tensions of should or should not, ought to or ought not, and resting in natural resilience, slips beyond the waves of suffering, struggle, and doubt."

The Bodhisattva understands that the way things are is the only way they could be, otherwise they would be different. We may wish things could have been different or hope that they will improve in the future, but none of this changes the way things actually are. To the extent we resist what is and the way in which we are participating in what is, to that extent we find ourselves in conflict, neuroses, and stucknesses for which we might seek therapy.

After all, isn't the goal of therapy self change? And isn't the function of the therapist to be a "change agent?" However, if we look closely at the notion of therapeutic change, we see a sleight of hand. As it is typically approached and practiced, psychotherapy is a heroic quest: we like to think that we are getting somewhere and making progress. Yet, while striving for progress, our innate capacity for resilience is easily eclipsed. We lose touch with subjective presence when we objectify our client as someone who needs to be improved upon. Following from this, we want change, but only change for the better. This is precisely what turns out to be impossible. In order to progress, it is usually necessary to regress; to successfully come to terms with a difficult life situation, we must embrace the difficulty of that situation. We must take it warmly into our arms and make it our own, otherwise we remain on the outside looking in.

Therapy is often framed in a language of redemption. We might "regress," but it would be "in the service of the ego" or "in the service of transcendence" (Washburn 1988). In either case, we envision therapy in terms of personal progress. But this is a sleight of hand. As the Bodhisattva knows, in deep, liberating therapy, there is no progress, no regress, and at bottom nothing to change, things finally being inhabited exactly as they are. If there was somewhere to progress to, where would that be? If we think it is somewhere other than where we are, how could we ever get there

here and now? And, if we think that it is here and now, then of course there is nowhere to progress to.

Taking life *as is*, without either confirming the solidity of things at their face value or disconfirming things as they appear, allows us to more directly and honestly inhabit the life in which we find ourselves. Releasing the aggressive preoccupation of trying to change the other or oneself loosens the conviction (even if it is a damnable conviction) in a dysfunctional, deficient "you/me," and enables the emergence of a compassionate, intelligent responsiveness.

The Bodhisattva understands that the way things are is the way they are not. *What is* is always already changing into what it is not. There is no need to seek change, since it is already happening. Ironically, trying to change can be the very thing that winds up impeding change. Either ignoring or remaining fixated on familiar problems and shortcomings perpetuates them, just as it allows for the emergence of resilient reckoning. Since resilience can only come from non-resilience, from resistance of some kind, it is by opening to whatever is resisted, feared, unwanted, or despised that it is able to be released. Empathic attunement, therapeutic courage (Bradford, 2001), insightful discernment, and steadfast accompaniment in providing a safe holding environment, or relational home (Stolorow, 2011), are a few of the skilful means that are conducive to eliciting resilience. There is nothing to change or to improve about one's client (or oneself) and no therapeutic progress to be made.

Only, the therapeutic play is that of being broken-open, perhaps in trembling, to the *wonderment* of being in the world.

Notes

1. This is a paraphrase of Chogyal Namkhai Norbu (1994, p.13).

2. See Adams, 1995, for a discussion of the congruencies between Phenomenological, Psychoanalytic, and Buddhist meditative attitudes.

3. Thich Nhat Hanh deserves credit for having coined this excellent term.

4. See the writings of Tulku Orgyen (1999 & 2000) and Tsoknyi Rinpoche (2003) for a more indepth explication of mind's cognizant nature, *tsal-wa*.

5. Thanks to Peter Fenner for translating this superb phrase.

References

Adams, W. (1995). Revelatory openness wedded with the clarity of unknowing: Psychoanalytic evenly suspended attention, the phenomenological attitude, and meditative awareness. *Psychoanalysis and Contemporary Thought, 18*(4), 463-494.

Atwood, G. & Stolorow, R. (1984). *Structures of subjectivity.* Hillsdale, N.J.: The Analytic Press.

Bennett, S, (1978). *Mind and madness in ancient Greece: The classical roots of modern psychiatry.* Ithaca, NY: Cornell Univ. Press.

Berger, P., & Luckmann, T. (1967). *The social construction of reality: A treatise in the sociology of knowledge.* New York, NY: Doubleday.

Boss, M. (1978). Eastern and Western therapy. In, J. Welwood (Ed.), *The meeting of the ways* (pp. 183-191). New York, NY: Schocken.

Boss, M. (1982). *Psychoanalysis and Daseinsanalysis.* DaCapo. (Original work published in 1963)

Boss, M. (1983). *Existential foundations of medicine and psychology.* New York, NY: Jason Aronson.

Bradford, G. K. (1989). The psychological transition to fatherhood: A phenomenological inquiry. Unpublished doctoral dissertation. Saybrook Institute, San Francisco, CA.

Bradford, G. K. (2001). Therapeutic courage. *Voices, 37*(2), 4-13.

Bradford, G. K. (2007). From neutrality to the play of unconditional presence. In, Prendergast, J. J. & Bradford, G. K. (Eds).

Listening from the heart of silence: Nondual   wisdom   and psychotherapy, Vol. 2. St. Paul, MN: Paragon House.

Bugental, J. (1965). *The search for authenticitiy: An existential-analytic approach to psychotherapy.* New York, NY: Holt, Rinehart & Winston.

Bugental, J. (1978). *Psychotherapy and process.* New York, NY: Addison-Wesley.

Chodron, P. (1997). *When things fall apart: Heart advice for difficult times.* Boston, MA: Shambhala.

Fenner, P. (2002). *The edge of certainty: Dilemmas on the Buddhist path.* York Beach, Maine: Nicolas-Hays.

Ferrer, J. N. (2002). *Revisioning transpersonal theory.* Albany, NY: SUNY Press.

Foucault, M. (1965). *Madness and civilization: A history of insanity in the age of reason.* (R. Howard, Trans.). NY: Random House. (Originally published in 1961)

Freud, S. (1961). *Civilization and its discontents.* (J. Strachey, Trans.). New York, NY: Norton. (Originally published in 1930)

Gadamer, H.G. (1982). *Truth and method.* (G. Barden & J. Cumming, Trans.). New York, NY: Crossroad. (Original work published in 1960)

Gendlin, E. T. (1973a). Experiential phenomenology. In M. Natanson (Ed.), *Phenomenology and the social sciences* (pp. 281-319). Evanston, IL: Northwestern University Press.

Gendlin, E. T. (1973b). Experiential psychotherapy. In Corsini (Ed.), *Current psychotherapies.* Itasca, IL: Peacock.

Gendlin, E. T. (1978). *Focusing.* New York, NY: Bantam.

Germer, C. K., Siegel, R. D., & Fulton, P. R. (2005). *Mindfulness and psychotherapy.* New York, NY: Guilford.

Giorgi, A. (1970). *Psychology as a human science: A phenomenologically based approach.* New York, NY: Harper & Row.

Giorgi, A. (1985). *Phenomenological and psychological research.* Pittsburgh, PA: Duquense University Press.

Goldstein, M. & Goldstein, I. F. (1978). *How we know: An exploration of the scientific process.* New York, NY: Plenum.

Gurwitsch, A. (1964). *The field of consciousness.* Pittsburgh, PA: Duquense University Press. (Original work published 1957)

Heidegger, M. (1962). *Being and time.* New York, NY: Harper and Row. (Original work published 1927)

Heidegger, M. (1966). *Discourse on thinking.* (Trans. J. Anderson and E. H. Freund). New York, NY: Harper Colophon. (Original work published 1959)

Horwitz, A. V., & Wakefield, J. C. (2007). *The loss of sadness: How psychiatry transformed normal sorrow into depressive disorder.* New York, NY: Oxford University Press.

Husserl, E. (1962). *Ideas: General introduction to pure phenomenology.* Translated by W. R. B. Gibson. New York, NY: Collier. (Original work published 1913)

Husserl, E. (1964). *The phenomenology of internal time-consciousness.* (M. Heidegger, Ed., J. Churchill, Trans.). Bloomington: Indiana University Press. (Original work published 1928)

Husserl, E. (1970). *The crisis of European sciences and Transcendental*

Phenomenology (D. Carr, Trans.). Evanston, IL: Northwestern University Press. (Original work published 1954)

Hutchins, R. (2002). Gnosis: Beyond disease and disorder to a diagnosis inclusive of gifts and challenges. *Journal of Transpersonal Psychology, 34*(2), 101-114.

Idhe, D. (1977). *Experimental phenomenology: An introduction.* New York, NY: Capricorn.

Ingersoll, E. (2002). An integral approach for teaching and practicing diagnosis. *Journal of Transpersonal Psychology, 34*(2), 115-128.

Jacobs, D. H. & Cohen, D. (2009). Does "psychological dysfunction mean anything?: A criticical essay on pathology vs. agency. *Journal of Humanistic Psychology, 50*(3), 312-334.

James, W. (1922). *Essays in radical empiricism.* New York, NY: Longmans, Green & Co. (Original work published in 1912)

Jerry, P. A. (2003). Challenges in transpersonal diagnosis. *Journal of Transpersonal Psychology, 35*(1), 43-59.

Jung, C. G. (1969). The transcendent function. In, *The structure and dynamics of the psyche, The collected works of C. G. Jung, Vol. 8.* (Trans. R. F. C. Hull). Princeton, NJ: Princeton University Press. (Original work written in 1957)

Kruger, D. (1979). An introduction to phenomenological psychology. Pittsburgh, PA: Duquense University Press.

Laing, R. D. (1960). *The divided self.* London: Tavistock.

Laing, R. D. (1967). *The politics of experience.* New York, NY: Pantheon.

Laing, R. D. (1969). *The politics of the family and other essays.* New York, NY: Vintage.

Lajoie, D. H., & Shapiro, S. I. (1992). Definitions of transpersonal psychology: The first twenty-three years. *Journal of Transpersonal Psychology*, *24*(1), 79-98.

Loy, D. (1996). *Lack and transcendence: The problem of death and life in psychotherapy, existentialism, and Buddhism.* Atlantic Highlands, NJ: Humanities Press.

Luijpen, W. A. (1960). *Existential Phenomenology.* Pittsburgh, PA: Duquense University.

Lukoff, D. (1985). Diagnosis of mystical experiences with psychotic features. *Journal of Transpersonal Psychology*, *17*(2), 155-181.

Lukoff, D. (1988). Transpersonal perspectives on manic psychosis: Creative, visionary, and mystical states. *Journal of Transpersonal Psychology*, *20*(2), 111-139.

Lukoff, D., Lu, F., & Turner, R. (1998). From spiritual emergency to spiritual problem: The transpersonal roots of the new DSM-IV category. *Journal of Transpersonal Psychology*, *38*(2), 21-50.

Maslow, A. H. (1971). *The farther reaches of human nature.* New York, NY: Penguin.

May, R. (1958). Contributions of Existential psychology. In, *Existence*. Ed. May, Angel & Ellenberger. N.Y.: Simon & Schuster.

May, R., Angel, E. & Ellenberger, H. F. (1958). *Existence*. NY: Simon & Schuster.

Merleau-Ponty, M. (1962). *The phenomenology of perception.* Translated by C. Smith. London: Routledge & Kegan Paul.

Merleau-Ponty, M. (1963). *The structure of behavior.* (Trans. A. L.

Fisher). Boston, MA: Beacon. (Original work published 1942)

Namkhai Norbu. (1986). *The crystal and the way of light: Sutra, tantra and dzogchen*. New York, NY: Routledge.

Namkhai Norbu, C. (1994). *Buddhism and psychology*. Arcidosso, Italy: Shang Shung Edizioni.

Namkhai Norbu, C. & Clemente, A. (1999). *The supreme source: The fundamental tantra of dzogchen semde, kunjed gyalpo*. (Trans. A. Lukianowicz). Ithaca, NY: Snow Lion.

Olendzki, A. (2012). No-self 2.0. In, *Shambhala Sun*, November, 81-83.

Ortega y Gassett. (1985). *The revolt of the masses*. (Trans. A. Kerrigan). New York, NY: Norton. (First published in 1930)

PDM Task Force. (2006). *Psychodynamic diagnostic manual*. Silver Spring, MD: Alliance of Psychoanalytic Organizations.

Prendergast, J. J. & Bradford, G. K. (2007). *Listening from the heart of silence: Nondual wisdom and psychotherapy, Volume 2*. St. Paul, MN: Paragon House.

Prendergast, J. J. (2007). Spacious intimacy: Reflections on essential relationship, empathic resonance, projective identification, and witnessing. In, Prendergast, J. J. & Bradford, G. K. (Eds). *Listening from the heart of silence: Nondual wisdom and psychotherapy, Volume 2*. St. Paul, MN: Paragon House.

Reynolds, J. (2000). *Self-liberation through seeing with naked awareness*. Ithaca, NY: Snow Lion.

Rogers, C. R. (1961). *On becoming a person: A therapist's view of psychotherapy*. Boston, MA: Houghton Mifflin.

Schneider, K. J., Bugental, J. & Pierson, J. F. (2001). *The handbook of*

Humanistic Psychology: Leading edges in theory, research, and practice. London: Sage.

Schneider, K. J. (2004). *Rediscovery of awe: Splendor, mystery, and the fluid center of life.* St. Paul, MN: Paragon Press.

Schneider, K. (2008). *Existential-integrative psychotherapy: Guideposts to the core of practice.* New York, NY: Routledge.

Schneider, K. J. (2009). *Awakening to awe: Personal stories of profound transformation.* New York, NY: Jason Aronson.

Skinner, B. F. (1971). *Beyond freedom and dignity.* New York, NY: Random House.

Sovatsky, S. (1998). *Words from the soul.* Albany, NY: SUNY Press.

Spinelli, E. (1989). *The interpreted world: An introduction to Phenomenological psychology.* London: Sage.

Stolorow, R. & Atwood, G. (1992). *Contexts of being: The intersubjective foundations of psychological life.* Hillsdale, NJ: The Analytic Press.

Stolorow, R. (2007). *Trauma and existence: Autobiographical, psychoanalytic, and philosophical reflections.* Hillsdale, NJ: The Analytic Press.

Stolorow, R. (2011). *World, affectivity, trauma: Heidegger and post-Cartesian psychoanalysis.* New York, NY: Routledge.

Szasz, T. S. (1974). *The myth of mental illness: Foundations of a theory of personal conduct.* Revised Edition. New York, NY: Harper & Row.

Taylor, T. (2009). *A spirituality for brokenness: Discovering your deepest self in difficult times.* Woodstock, VT: Skylight Paths.

Trungpa, C. (2005). *The sanity we are born with: A Buddhist approach to psychology.* Boston, MA: Shambhala.

Tsoknyi, R. (2003). *Fearless simplicity: The dzogchen way of living feely in a complex world.* Boudhanath, Nepal: Rangjung Yeshe Publications.

Tulku Orgyen, R. (1999). *As it is, Volume 1.* Boudhanath, Nepal: Rangjung Yeshe.

Tulku Orgyen, R. (2000). *As it is, Volume 2.* Boudhanath, Nepal: Rangjung Yeshe.

Van den Berg, J. H. (1972). *A different existence: Principles of phenomenological psychopathology.* Pittsburgh, PA: Duquesne University Press.

Valle, R. & Halling, S. (1989). *Existential-Phenomenological perspectives in psychology.* New York, NY: Plenum.

Van den Berg, J. H. (1972). *A different existence: Principles of phenomenological psychopathology.* Pittsburgh: Duquense University Press.

Washburn, M. (1988). *The ego and the dynamic ground: A transpersonal theory of human development.* Albany, NY: SUNY.

Wegela, K. (1994). Contemplative psychotherapy: A path of uncovering brilliant sanity. *Journal of Contemplative Psychotherapy, 9,* 27-52.

Wegela, K. K. (2011). *What really helps: Using mindfulness & compassion presence to help, support, and encourage others.* Boston, MA: Shambhala.

Welwood, J. (2000). *Toward a psychology of awakening: Buddhism, psychotherapy, and the path of personal and spiritual transfor-mation.* Boston, MA: Shambhala.

Winnicott, D. W. (1971). *Playing and reality.* New York, NY: Tavistock.

Index